Letters from Law School
The Life of a Second-Year Law Student

Lawrence Dieker Jr.

Writers Club Press
San Jose New York Lincoln Shanghai

Letters from Law School
The Life of a Second-Year Law Student

All Rights Reserved © 2000 by Lawrence Dieker Jr.

Published by Writers Club Press
an imprint of iUniverse.com, Inc.

For information address:
iUniverse.com, Inc.
5220 S 16th, Ste. 200
Lincoln, NE 68512
www.iuniverse.com

ISBN: 0-595-00975-1

Printed in the United States of America

Epigraph

I gradually became aware that second-year and third-year students were moving through a world much different than that of a 1L.

Scott Turow, *One L*

Preface

Law students today have a pretty good idea what to expect their first year. Scott Turow's *One L*, describing his first year at Harvard, has become almost mandatory reading for anyone contemplating law school. And because that level of intensity is what so many expect, that is how the first year usually plays out, complete with ulcers, outlines, and relentless work.

But the education does not end after the first year.

Law school is a three-year course of study. There is more to law school than the initial shock of the plunge, and the first year often bears little resemblance to the final two. Still reeling in many ways from their first year, second-year law students face two more years of grueling work, mounting student loans, increasing pressure to distinguish themselves in some way from the crowd, and the never-ending search for the perfect job. Second-year law students come to realize that surviving the fall into the deep end does not guarantee they will be able to swim, let alone come up for air.

While the setting for much of this book is Tulane Law School, in New Orleans, Louisiana, one of the more outstanding law schools in the country, the characters and law firms described herein are either composites or products of my imagination. No character in this book should be confused with any real individual. No action, motive, description, or speech should be ascribed to any such individual, living or dead. This said, I do believe this book captures the experiences of an upper-class law student, if only from one person's perspective.

A few things
I just thought
You should know.

Lawrence Dieker Jr.
April 2000

Acknowledgements

Thanks to Tim O'Brien for his inspiration, Nolan Porterfield for his encouragement, and Scott Turow for his courage in blazing the trail.

1

"So how do you know Mr. Reese?" the lawyer asked me.

The truth: I didn't know Mr. Reese at all. A letter to him had landed me an interview with his law firm, Bradford & Bain, a mammoth law firm that occupied several floors of one of the newer office buildings towering over Capital Square in downtown Columbus, Ohio. While I was home to be married, I had lined up several interviews for the following summer. Bradford paid its summer associates something in excess of $20,000. A good job. A glamorous job. It might lead to an offer for full-time employment following graduation, and in any event it was certainly experience toward a full-time job, whatever awaited me beyond that black curtain at the end of three years of law school.

I knew Mr. Reese was a partner with the firm. But I could not have recognized him. We had never even spoken.

"He's a friend of the family," I said. But sounding out across the wide desk, the response had a feeble edge. The casual words seemed to get lost in the expanse between us. The lawyer looked at me a moment as if he were trying to make sense of the fragments. His eyes narrowed. With a flourish of his hand, he referred to a note attached to my resume.

"His son and your brother are friends?"

"That's right."

A tenuous connection, perhaps, but by no means ridiculous. I knew where Mr. Reese lived. I had picked up my brother from the house once. I had even delivered his newspaper as a substitute carrier. Mr. Reese liked his newspaper in his mailbox. It was a big metal box painted like a flag. I had been granted an interview, hadn't I? There was some connection.

But the lawyer, the chairman of the firm's hiring committee, was busy tossing other obstacles my way. In my rush to put my resume together, I had omitted details about the law firm where I had just spent the summer—Simoneaux, Troy & Walters—little details, like where the firm was located and how many attorneys it employed. The fact that Simoneaux was of comparable size, with more than a hundred attorneys, should have been a point in my favor, but the chairman let me know he found the presentation of my life confusing. He moved his finger along the page, searching. He stumbled over words and looked at the ceiling, balancing my future like a ball on the tip of his nose.

"What type of law do you think you'd like to practice?" he asked, finally. "Perhaps it's too early to tell."

"I think I'd make a good insurance litigator," I told him. On this point I felt prepared. The night before I had looked up Bradford & Bain in Martindale-Hubbell, a directory of lawyers and law firms, to get a sense of the firm's primary practice areas, the background of some of the firm's attorneys, the credentials of recent hires. One question that came up frequently during interviews was what type of law the student might want to practice. Law students who sit and stare out the window with no concept of the future, no career goals to speak of, without mentioning so much as a class they particularly enjoyed, are adrift in the water.

Bradford & Bain seemed to have a basic corporate practice. With my liberal arts degree, in English, corporate law was something I always had trouble embracing with any apparent conviction. My connection, Mr. Reese, was, among other things, a member of the Ohio Insurance Association. Bradford & Bain probably represented the insurance industry. That was okay. I had done some insurance litigation work over the summer at the Simoneaux law firm. Strong points exist on both sides. Industry cannot be an insurer for every injury tangentially related to its products; on the other hand, there are some very injured people out there …

He let me explain, encouraging me whenever we made eye contact, his eyes flashing.

When he was certain I had finished, he said, "We don't really do much insurance litigation here."

I struggled to understand. I felt as if I had been hit. Dizzy, I tried to regain my balance. Wasn't this Bradford & Bain? Mr. Reese? The Ohio Insurance Association? One thing was certain: The interview was over. I didn't imagine that flash of satisfaction, quickly contained. The chairman reached toward his pocket for something, thought better of it, started to rise, but readjusted himself and crossed his legs instead. I hadn't moved. I hadn't breathed. I couldn't. I was still upright. If he wanted to knock me down, I thought, he would have to do better than that.

"The smaller firms in town tend to do the insurance-related work," he went on, and as he spoke I realized with a gulp that he had knocked the air out of me and I was falling of my own accord. "You should try a firm like Ravetz, Liskoff. They do a lot of insurance litigation. Have you applied with them?"

I shook my head.

A few minutes later, as he escorted me down the hallway to the elevator, I made a last desperate attempt to continue the interview: "Where do the clerks work?"

The sound of my voice seemed to take him by surprise. He winked involuntarily at another lawyer waiting for the elevator.

I pressed on, momentarily revived. "Where I worked last summer all the clerks worked in a room off the library." It was pointless, but I went on anyway.

"The clerks have offices," he said. "Usually two clerks will share an office."

I tried to seem interested. He had to appreciate the effort. Stepping off the elevator, he paused to show me the firm's famous boardroom. We looked in from the hallway. A cavernous room, high ceiling, portraits on the walls, dominated by a giant round table of dark polished wood. But before I could absorb the whole scene, the door was closed and we were moving again down the hall. The giant table, the portraits, the tradition, power, prestige, all vanished before my eyes.

The problem was I had no idea what the future held. But I couldn't just blurt out to the chairman of the law firm's hiring committee that my future was uncertain, that I had at best some vague notion that I would do ... whatever it was lawyers did. My secretary would sit behind walls somewhere outside my door. My lunches would be scheduled. My kids would come to visit, marvel at the frosted glass, and run like orphans through the halls ...

During my interview with Gaines, Duncan, Duffy & Gray, a few days before, I had paused so long to ponder the question, ponder my future, that one of the lawyers excused herself. And Gaines, where I had worked in the library the summer prior to starting law school, the law firm that handled my uncle's legal affairs, had been one of my best prospects for landing a job back in Columbus. Where did I see myself in five years? The reels spun. I waited. They waited. The world waited. Someone somewhere was talking. Why was it now so quiet? Fuzz. The tape was erased. Nothing. No words. Only fuzz. The essays you write for the law school admissions office, I quickly discovered, just do not sound convincing when spoken: nobility of the profession, benevolence, social consciousness, fascination with the law, omnipresence of the law.... It sounded like an empty tin can hitting the floor. No ring to it at all. Besides, you would have to be an idiot to believe half of those things.

These people were all tall.

They were all attractive.

They all looked alike.

I was short, plain, African, Asian, German, Indian, Hispanic, English, overweight, unsure, undefined, and unimaginable.

With a strong toothy smile, they all wanted to know what I was doing there, taking up their time. Why do you want to be a lawyer? Perhaps it's too early to tell.

Gaines had been one of my best chances for landing a job in Columbus. And now I had missed my opportunity with Bradford & Bain.

August 15
(Thursday)

My final interview in Columbus before returning to Tulane Law School, in New Orleans, Louisiana, was with Brunnett & Carne, a firm with offices in Columbus, Cleveland, and Washington, D.C. With no guarantee from the Gaines law firm, and my chances at Bradford & Bain doubtful, I double-checked all my facts. I wanted very much to return to Columbus the following summer. If I was to avoid flying back to Columbus for more interviews during the school year, this firm was my final chance.

And from the start, Brunnett & Carne seemed to take me seriously. While I had become used to meeting with associates whose job, I finally decided, was to see if I reminded them of themselves, at Brunnett, I met with partners right from the start, two partners and two associates from the hiring committee over the course of a morning. I was also leaner, meaner. I was now more familiar with the kinds of questions being asked of second-year students, more rehearsed with my answers. And with several misfires behind me, I was a little desperate. This could be my last chance.

I had questions.

They had answers.

Brunnett & Carne was perhaps best known outside the legal community for representing the Stromburg family in business and divorce matters. By the time I walked into the final interview, I was thinking I just might be around next summer for an invitation to Stromburg Farms, where the family's thoroughbreds are trained and where two World Series trophies are on display, guarded by a crack security staff and a stuffed prowling panther. The final interview was with a middle-aged patent attorney, a graduate of Northwestern Law School. The diploma was the only thing on his wall. My resume was the only thing on his desk. He was bald with a thick mustache and, from the moment I was shown into his office, seemed bent on discovering how, with law students wandering the land like refugees, I had gotten a summer job at Simoneaux, Troy & Walters, the ancient New Orleans firm where I had just spent the past ten weeks.

"How is the job market in New Orleans?" he wanted to know.

I admitted that it was bad, that I had been lucky. He waited for more. "My grades improved dramatically my second semester," I explained.

To many interviewers, rising grades would have shown a certain adaptability, that I was a quick study, full of potential. But to an old lawyer, an experienced detective, someone who could smell blood, my explanation was an admission that my grades had been merely mediocre after my first semester, which made my job at Simoneaux even more of a mystery. One Ls interview in the spring on the strength of their first semester grades. If the grades aren't in, they occasionally interview on the strength of their LSAT score. He understood the situation immediately.

"How was your LSAT score?" he asked.

"One fifty-nine," I admitted. It was hard to admit. I could have said one sixty-one. Perhaps I should have. There was no way he could have known differently. But I blurted out the truth: One fifty-nine. It wasn't a terrible score. It had placed me in the top twenty percent of those who had taken the test, presumably a pretty intelligent group. Largely on the strength of that score, I had been accepted to a number of good schools: Villanova, Case Western, Marquette, Tulane. All the same, I had the feeling, as he scratched the number with sharp strokes across the top of my resume, that, contrary to what he later told me, I would not be given every consideration when the hiring committee convened later that month.

2

My wife, Katie, and I were married in the interval between my summer internship and my return to Tulane for my second year of law school, shortly after a frantic group of interviews that seemed to fizzle like faulty fireworks. After a short honeymoon down the East Coast, we took an apartment over a po-boy shop on St. Charles Avenue in New Orleans. Big trucks on the street made the place bounce like it was on box springs, the streetcar rattled all night long, and the family next door kept five dogs and an enormous white rooster that crowed three perfect notes at irregular intervals throughout the day. On the edge of the Garden District, we thought we were putting some distance between ourselves and the law school, but we found ourselves surrounded by law students. Two of my classmates were living in the building across the street. A 1L named Howard Sloan moved in across the hall.

Those first few days, while Katie unpacked her things, I sat in the living room reading letters that had gathered while I was away, responses to the job letters I had sent to law firms before going home in hopes of lining up interviews while I was in Columbus. *Dear Mr. Westphal: Thank you for writing. Please do not write again.* Many students learn quickly to skim these letters for the "thank you again" or the "best of luck." I lingered. It was morbid, a bit like lingering over a corpse, but I couldn't help it. One letter, though, did hold some promise. It was from Fielding & Watt, a firm, like Gaines, that did work for my uncle's company. I hadn't heard back from them before my trip to Ohio, but at least they were still keeping me in mind:

> Dear Mr. Westphal:
>
> Harry Canton of our office has forwarded your letter of July 6, with attached resume to our Recruiting Committee. Our Recruiting Committee has reviewed the material you sent us. Your qualifications are impressive. Therefore, the Recruiting Committee would like to hold on to your resume for further review.
>
> Thank you for your interest in our firm. We will be in touch with you shortly.
>
> > Sincerely,
> >
> > Claudette Villiere
> > Recruiting Coordinator

I added the letter to a small stack of papers in the corner of my desk, names of Tulane graduates in Ohio, information on law firms I thought of as potential job prospects.

August 25
(Sunday)

Rosey Land, a 2L, and her brother Gerard, a 3L, threw a party Sunday night to welcome everyone back. Their apartment was on Royal Street in the French Quarter, a few blocks from the market, and, like many of the apartments in the Quarter, something of an oasis behind high walls and shutters. Most people gathered in the courtyard around a pool shared by several surrounding apartment units. Students splashed fully clothed while one of the neighbors slowly did his evening laps.

Rosey's landlord, a judge, was in the courtyard preaching to the converted that law school should be at most a two-year program. And the more he drank, the more aggressively he expounded the view that law school was just business as usual, a way to take money from one person's pocket and put it in another's.

"The only secret to thinking like a lawyer," he said, "is thinking your time is worth two hundred and fifty bucks an hour."

"Robert Bork bills out at five hundred an hour," a 3L said.

"What Bork provides for five hundred an hour you don't learn in law school."

At the tables near the other end of the courtyard we found Jonathan Berck, one of our new neighbors, sitting beneath a camellia tree, taking in the scene. Jonathan was also a 2L, a sociology major from UCLA.

"You've got a new look, I see," I told him. He didn't understand at first. It was the same old Jonathan, blue jeans and ponytail, but now he wore a pair of thick black-rimmed glasses. "Those glasses, they look great. You look somehow smarter than before."

"Cheaper than law school," he said.

"You don't need to go to law school at all with those glasses."

Kevin St. Germain and his wife, Lesley, were nearby. Both had evidently been at the party for some time. They knew who was where, what to eat, and when the Jacuzzi would be free. Kevin was also a 2L, an accounting major from Madison, Wisconsin. I asked Kevin about his summer, and he told me that he was on the Maritime Law Journal. This was news. Becoming a member of a law journal was one of the ways to distinguish one's self in law school, almost a prerequisite to a job at the larger firms. This was great news.

He nodded toward the camellia tree. "So's Jonathan."

I looked to my left where Jonathan was sitting in the shade. He had heard our discussion, and looked at me with his big glasses, a little

shrug as if to say, it just didn't come up.... They were both on the
Maritime Law Journal. That was something of a shock. Both of them.
That made a difference somehow. Others were succeeding, and I hadn't
even made the attempt. At the close of spring semester the previous
year, the Maritime Law Journal had distributed materials for its "write
on" competition. Using only these materials, applicants were to write a
detailed examination of a judicial opinion called a "casenote." Those
writing the best casenotes would be asked to join the staff. The prospect
of being on a legal journal was exciting, and I had thought about it
occasionally throughout the summer. Still, the deadline snuck up on
me. The night before the casenote was due, I spread the materials on the
dining room table and read a couple of the cases. It was ten o'clock
before I knew it. I made some notes. Soon it was two o'clock. I had to
work the next day. I had a good job at Simoneaux. The job might lead
somewhere. I didn't need journal experience. And there was always the
Law Review competition in the fall. I would work doubly hard then.
Law Review was the big prize. The Maritime Law Journal was just one
of the smaller satellites. Besides, I was tired, so tired I could hardly keep
my eyes open ...

Now I could see I had made a mistake. People were getting ahead. I was
being left behind, left out, lost. There would be meetings, discussions after
class, references others just couldn't understand or appreciate. Never
mind. Not worth repeating. I stood in the courtyard trying to think, lost
in thought, nodding vaguely in the direction of an old camellia tree.

3

Our Evidence professor was already at the front of the room, leaning against the table, watching the seats fill up over the top of his wrinkled notes. Maurice Landrow. A little man with red hair, short-cropped beard, and suspenders. At first I didn't believe this dapper little man could be our Evidence professor. He seemed to genuinely enjoy being there, among the students. He seemed to be grinning. I was used to seeing law professors enter at the stroke of the hour, head down. Professor Pillsbury, my first-year Civil Procedure professor, used to pace the halls rather than stand behind the lectern before class for even two terrible minutes. Landrow looked like he couldn't wait to get started.

"I heard him complaining in the hall about the new grading curve," Barb Griffith told me as we settled into our seats.

The new grading curve required professors to award 60 percent of the class a grade of "B" or better, up from 45 percent the previous year.

"He said pretty soon he'd have to give everyone an A."

Although Dean Gottlieb was fond of saying that every student at Tulane, every member of the class, from top to bottom, was qualified to step into work at one of the large law firms, partners at those firms, as one told me, well, they didn't quite believe that. Landrow was a partner at one of the largest firms in the city, an adjunct professor, someone who taught to keep his skills sharp and to raise his stature in the legal community. Of course, like Landrow, many adjunct professors obviously love to teach. Grade inflation likely bothered him for several reasons.

Around the room I saw the familiar faces, a little older, a little wearier, a number with worry now sprouting from their heads in coarse white strands. Rosey was right. We were survivors. We had glimpsed the abyss and held fast. Others had turned back, walking away with their arms swinging at their sides, their coats flapping in the breeze. Lighter, much lighter, God how much lighter, but still somewhere deep the faintest little bit of heaviness, almost imperceptible. No former law student can ever leave law school completely behind. They could never be rid of what brought them there in the first place. They would carry it forever.

By nine o'clock, almost all of the seats in the lecture hall were filled, more than 140 students. Evidence was a popular course, required in many schools. A lawyer is expected to know something about the Rules of Evidence. When people think about lawyers, they usually conjure up images of the courtroom, the lawyer rising to speak.

—Objection, your Honor. Hearsay.

—Sustained.

Most lawyers see little of the courtroom, but a practical reason existed for taking the course: the Rules of Evidence were also on virtually every state's bar exam. Students may do fine in law school. They may do better than fine. But if they do not pass a three-day exam two months after graduation, they would never be lawyers. So while first year students worry about surviving law school, second year students begin to worry about the rest of their life, how they would pay off their student loans, how their education would translate into a career, and what they would need to know to pass the bar exam.

"There was this LAWYER," Landrow shouted, signaling the start of class. The room settled down. Some people giggled. He was telling a joke. How corny. Landrow told one about the big city lawyer whose practice took him to a farm. Walking through the cow pasture, the lawyer stepped in some manure. The farmer found the lawyer standing there, screaming.

"Why, you just stepped in a little cow dropping," the farmer told him.

"Thank goodness," the lawyer said. "I thought I was melting."

Some students smiled, others laughed politely.

"Hey," Landrow said, tugging at his suspenders. "It's your chosen profession."

Landrow's semester reading looked pretty demanding, about 600 pages. But while most law books are filled with cases to be diagnosed and discussed, the Evidence book was basically an exposition of the law. Evidence class would therefore be somewhat atypical; we would spend class time working the problems at the end of each chapter. In most classes, professors are content to cover four- or five-hundred pages of legal cases in some depth, a method of study that allows students to see how the law works, to see the reasoning behind the rules, to debate humanistic values versus economic efficiency, good versus bad, white versus black. With a variety of commercial outlines, briefs, and law summaries on the market, professors wouldn't be asking much of students merely to replicate what was already available for less than $30. After all, a good lawyer is one who can comprehend and interpret the law. The law is ever-evolving, ever-changing. A good law school teaches you to think. Rules come and go, but conceptual tools will always serve you well ...

Still, when news got out during our first year that less than 70 percent of Tulane law students had passed the Louisiana bar exam, students were suddenly concerned. Spending $65,000 on tuition, many expected to know at least enough law to pass the bar. Professors, especially those with more theoretical approaches, were on the defensive. Tulane's free-market

approach to class selection was under attack. The administration
scheduled a meeting with students to discuss course selection. The old
explanations about the purposes of a legal education were hauled out
and presented by several of the school's more respected professors. The
bar exam, that final hurdle, was put into perspective. Yes, the bar exam
was something to consider when scheduling classes. No, we should not
plan our entire law school education around the subjects tested on a
state's bar exam.

"Taking the *bah* exam is like having to tap dance," Professor Pillsbury
told us, finally. "It bears about as much relation to law school.... The
bah review course will teach you everything you need to know to pass."

For many, though, the thought of paying $600 for Tulane's bar
review course seemed like one more bitter pill to swallow.

Over the next couple of classes, Landrow would introduce us to the
basics of trying a case. Pre-trial preparation, he said, was the most
important part. As lawyers, we would always have to keep three things
in mind: the facts we would need to prove, the witnesses who would
get those facts before the jury, and the exhibits we would introduce
with each witness. Landrow was so enthusiastic, we were all ready to
give it a try. Get the videotape running. Competence is preparation.
You only have to be fifty-one percent right to get one hundred percent
of your damages ...

*   *   *

I had a couple of hours before Business Enterprises, or "B.E.," as it
was called, so I went to the bookstore to see if my other books were in.
Like everything else associated with the law, the price of books has continued to rise over the years. In 1975, Scott Turow plunked down $16
for a casebook. Today, casebooks typically cost between $40 and $60,
which means the average student can spend $200 each semester on
assigned books alone. No one likes paying that kind of money, but I was

astounded to discover that one of the books for Landrow's class, a book Landrow himself had written, was priced at $95. I checked several copies to be sure.

"This can't be right," I said to a girl taking books out of a box and stacking them on a shelf. She volunteered to check. A few minutes later she came back and said, yes, that was right: $95. I found another law student, Alex Sarkis. He was taking Evidence as well. "Can you believe this?" I showed him the book.

"I've seen," he said.

"It's outrageous."

"You don't have to buy it," he said. "It's optional."

I looked at the reading list taped to the shelf. It didn't say "optional."

"I heard Landrow say something to some people after class," Alex told me.

"The professor's own book is not optional," I said.

Even worse than the initial price of books, though, was the depreciation once they were driven off the lot. At the end of last year, I decided I didn't want to lug my old casebooks from one place to another the rest of my life. It wasn't necessary. I had my class notes. I had the commercial outlines. If I needed to research the law, I could always go to the library. So I gathered all my old books, loaded the car, and took them to Tulane's bookstore, where, when I stacked them on the buyback counter, a nice young lady asked me quietly if I knew how much I would get for used books. I had counted on at least $100, perhaps $150. Getting half of my cost back would be ideal.

"I can give you five dollars a book," she told me.

"Five dollars!"

"Nobody wants to buy used law books," she explained.

"Used law books are the best kind. They've already got answers to questions in the margins and highlight material the professor thinks is important."

"Most law students want new books."

So I loaded the books back in the car and took them to Loyola's bookstore. Loyola University was where my wife, Katie, went to school. Its campus was right next to Tulane's, which was one of the reasons we had come to New Orleans.

"How much can I get for these books?" I asked the man in charge. He referred to a thick paperback guide and began quoting me the going rates. Several of my books he couldn't buy back because the publisher was overstocked. Some were already outdated. Others I sold for between $8 and $13.

Well, I thought, at least I was getting the going rates.

*   *   *

Professor Tarenzella, the B.E. instructor, entered the classroom at precisely one o'clock. A tall woman in loose-fitting clothes, she shut the door behind her, and, whenever someone straggled in late, stopped speaking until the student walked up the steps, down the aisle, found a seat, spread out books and papers and pens and looked up to see why everyone was so quiet. "I'll tolerate this today," she told us after several delays, "but being late doesn't just interrupt me, it interrupts the whole class." Then another student entered and the silence would begin again.

A graduate of the University of Iowa and former associate at Baker & McKenzie, in Washington, D.C., Tarenzella rattled off the topics of the course in businesslike fashion: corporations, partnerships, sole proprietorships, limited partnerships, *ultra vires* ...

"This stuff is cake," a fellow behind me said early in the semester.

A number of people in the class seemed comfortable with our first few discussions on various business enterprises, and I worried a little initially that my liberal arts background would put me at a disadvantage to the business majors and certified public accountants in the room. The year before in Constitutional Law I'd had a similar fear of political science majors. Their only real advantage, it turned out, was that they caught on a little more quickly. Things evened up as the course went along. That thought wasn't much consolation, though, when everyone else seemed to understand the tax consequences of choosing the corporate business form, and with every question Tarenzella was getting closer and closer to me.

The exam, she announced that first day, would be closed book.

Some members of the class objected.

"Can we bring the statute?" someone asked from the back of the room. We had purchased a thick paperback containing the Revised Model Business Corporation Act, the Model Close Corporation Supplement, the Uniform Partnership Act, the Uniform Limited Partnership Act, the Revised Uniform Limited Partnership Act, numerous federal securities laws, assorted corporation forms, and general corporation law from California, Delaware, Indiana, Maryland, New York, Pennsylvania, and Wyoming.

"You can bring your statute," she said.

But not everyone was pleased.

"I'm still considering an open note exam," she admitted, "but for the time-being count on it being closed book."

Some students wanted more details. "Can we write in the margins?"

"No."

The class grumbled uneasily.

A moment later, Tarenzella seemed to reconsider. "You can't write anything in the margin beyond the ordinary type of margin notes."

It didn't seem to be her final word on the subject.

By the end of class, Tarenzella got around to calling on someone from the class roster. "Rachel Grimes? Is Ms. Grimes here?"

No answer.

"Leo Gutters?"

There was the sound of pain from the center of the room.

Tarenzella asked a question that seemed to have something to do with contracts. It sounded familiar, like something I should have known. Mr. Gutters seemed a bit flustered as well.

"Do you remember Contracts One?" she asked.

"That was a long time ago," said Mr. Gutters.

People laughed.

"Can anyone help Mr. Gutters?"

Someone did, but by then books were starting to close. Class dismissed.

Tommy Wong found me after class. "I'll sit over here next time," he said. Tarenzella had promised to pass around a seating chart then. Tommy was an older student, a former high school biology teacher, who had been in several of my classes the previous year. His wife, Miko, was a paralegal at one of the large downtown firms. I had seen her occasionally over the summer on the street waiting for her ride, and we always promised to get together. With low grades and increasing doubts about his decision to study law, that first year had been especially hard on Tommy. One of the few comforts during his initial brush with the law, it seemed, was that he no longer dissected frogs. He said as much numerous times, and Miko always laughed enough at the explanation to seem implicated somehow in the decision.

"So what do you think?" I asked him. I wanted to know what he thought about Tarenzella.

He shrugged. "She's all right, I guess. Say, you want to work part-time? I need to find someone. I'm cutting back to about ten hours a week, and I need someone to work the other ten to fifteen hours."

I thought about it a moment. Tommy worked for a small New Orleans firm. Mostly clerical work. The pay wasn't great. It wouldn't help me get back to Ohio. Besides, I had to stay focused on the important matters. Interview season and the Law Review competition would absorb huge amounts of my time, and grades, as always, would be one of the most important indicia of my future success. Too much was at stake, so I said something about my heavy workload and left it at that.

August 27
(Tuesday)

On Tuesdays and Thursdays, I attended Remedies, Federal Practice, and Pollution Control. While Evidence and B.E. were classes taken by almost every law student, the remainder of my schedule was not so common. Like many schools, Tulane placed no restrictions on the class selection of upper-class students. I had signed up for Remedies because Professor Bonfante, my Torts professor, had suggested the course. "Clients don't care about the law," he told us. "They want to know how much money they can get."

My professor for Remedies was Nathan Worth, and as he introduced a course that would focus on the policies behind various remedies rather than mortality tables, it became clear that Worth and Bonfante had very different ideas about how Remedies should be taught.

I should have expected as much. Worth was my academic advisor and had been my Legal Research and Writing instructor the year before. This was his second year at Tulane. A University of Chicago Law School graduate, Worth had practiced law in New York for several years before choosing the professorial route. Students who had him the year before commented on his quirkiness and his poor attendance record. Some found significance in the fact that on the first day of class he read them a joke straight from a book.

"Why did you leave the practice of law?" a member of my writing group asked him at our first meeting.

"It's a fair question," he said, and proceeded to describe the practice of law as he saw it. I had the sensation of being at the bottom a dark pit with slick steel walls stretching to the sky.

As the semester wore on, Worth's enmity toward the legal profession was never far from the surface. He went through class tossing barbs at students who expected to be millionaires by the age of thirty or who amassed tens of thousands in debt because they heard that "lawyers

make lots of money." In class, he didn't require preparation or participation. He didn't even require attendance. If we left a note on his lectern
before class, he wouldn't bother calling on us at all. In fact, he gave the
impression that almost anything would be a more productive use of our
time than going to law school. He embraced the law like an arranged
marriage, and taught the most emotionally charged courses—such as
Family Law and Remedies, courses that lent themselves to heady discussions of right and wrong—with obvious detachment to a room full
of empty seats.

I realized when I walked into Remedies that first day that I had forgotten to pick up a mimeographed case we were supposed to have read.
I asked Jose Cadicamo, a friend from Civil Procedure the year before, if
he had a copy.

"We were supposed to pick up a case?" Jose said.

It soon became clear that we weren't the only ones unprepared.
"Many of you haven't read it," Worth said. "I know because there's still
a stack of them in my office." He seemed resigned. "Yes, I know, reading
cases is for *first-year* students."

We all thought that was pretty funny. No doubt that was how many
felt. Having been through so much our first year, something had to give,
and it might as well be the daily grind of reading. I made a note to pick
up the case, though, and planned to read it the first chance I got.

*   *   *

From Remedies I went straight to Federal Practice, a class I
expected to drop from my schedule. Already I felt spread thin, but my
Pollution Control class was starting to worry me. Earlier that morning I was reading the syllabus Professor Muder had posted in the hall
when I noticed Jonathan Berck looking over my shoulder. I pointed to
the lengthy reading assignments.

"I've seen it," Jonathan said. "Look." He pointed to a section of the syllabus with more than two dozen cases listed.

"Wow."

"I've read them already."

"Really?"

Jonathan laughed. "Just kidding."

For class, we would have to purchase a book of environmental law statutes, a casebook, and a thick supplement put together by Professor Muder. The supplement had a red cover. No powder blue here, not even environmental green, just blood red.

Having to wade through both a casebook and a supplement seemed daunting. We would be responsible for 291 pages of the casebook, I figured. The supplement, filled with case studies, case law, newspaper clippings, law review articles, and Muder's own witticisms, including a long poem she had written, brought the reading to 659 pages. Wow. For a moment, Muder almost had me in her grasp. I had that fleeting feeling that I was part of something great, something hard but worthwhile, something character-building and nation-bettering and triumphant. This was law school. They scare you to death the first year, work you to death the second, and bore you to death the third. People dream about going to law school, about becoming lawyers. I was realizing the dream, hard but fine. This was a new beginning. This was the year I would make something of myself.... Then I realized to my horror that my calculating hadn't taken into account the environmental law statutes themselves, pages and pages of fine print on finger-licking thin pages.

The woman herself did nothing to calm my fears. That first day Rita Muder stood before us mumbling dissatisfaction that her greeting had not been met with a rousing return.

"Let's try it again," she said to the class. "Good AFTERNOON."

"GOOD AFTERNOON," we responded.

She nodded. Muder had an almost saintly appearance—thin, austere, hard, simple, sure, and very frightening. Students either loved or hated her, but few disputed her ability to teach. A former U.S. army computer scientist, she made a name for herself after law school forcing the cleanup of a scenic valley where thousands of barrels containing chemical residues had been dumped, left to rust, leak, and contaminate.

"I came to Louisiana ten years ago to help clean up the leaking underground storage tanks along the Bayou," she told us early in the semester, nodding her head. "I'm still here."

But hazardous waste law would be reserved for another course. The primary thrust of Pollution Control would be the Federal Water Pollution Control Act, more commonly called the Clean Water Act or, as my notes would say, the CWA.

"You should know enough about the Clean Water Act to take a client," Muder said, a comment aimed, I decided, at the practitioners in the room. Under the direction of Professor Edward Oswald, a wetlands expert, Tulane's environmental law program was becoming one of the better known programs in the nation. Professors such as Rita Muder helped. Recently, Tulane had begun to offer a master's degree in Energy and Environmental Law. As a consequence, Pollution Control was filled with older students who came to class wearing suits or suspenders, carrying briefcases, and flashing fancy fountain pens.

But the master of law program was only one reason a class that had recently been a seminar of 20 students now filled the largest classroom in the school. What had attracted me to the class, like so many others, was the school's recent offering of a "Certificate of Specialization in Environmental Law," a specialty earned by taking 15 hours of environmental and administrative law classes. With the ever-narrowing job market, law schools across the country were attempting to develop specialties to help distinguish their students. In addition to environmental law, Tulane offered certificates in maritime law and international law. A specialty would presumably help to set a student apart—especially, it seemed to me, a specialty in environmental law, which was, after all, a "hot" field. All the legal publications said so.

Besides, as one of the students in the class said early in the semester, "Being forced to read some of the most difficult statutes ever written must surely have some intrinsic value."

I tried to agree.

Muder introduced us to Pollution Control with questions fired about the room like artillery shells, a pattern she would repeat almost every class. "Say a coal-fired power plant were being built in your state," she said. "What are the environmental impacts? What permits are required? Are the emissions hazardous? How does one decide if the plant gets a permit? Some fish will die. How many? Who decides? Why regulate at all? Why not let people sue in nuisance? Why not rely on free market forces?"

And we were off.

*   *   *

That afternoon, the Law Review held a meeting to kick off its annual writing competition. People are generally selected for Law Review on the basis of their first-year grades. At Tulane, the top 7.5 percent—twenty-two people in my class—were invited to join after the second semester grades were posted. During the summer at Simoneaux, I watched as several of my fellow first-year clerks received the coveted invitation to join. This was, I could tell, a distinction sweet to the taste.

About a hundred students filled the room to hear about the competition. A student who sat in front of me wore a tee shirt that said, "Make Love, Not Law Review." I figured he was covered either way. And one by one, the editors of the Law Review encouraged us to make the effort. Although only six people would be invited to join, in the previous year a scant forty had turned in casenotes at the close of the competition. "That makes your chances of being selected pretty good," the senior managing editor said. Two important points: The competition was to be strictly confidential, and the deadline for turning in papers was inflexible. This last point was belabored.

The competition itself seemed rather straightforward. We could choose one of four approved cases on which to write. The casenote would be made up of five sections: Overview of the Case, Background, The Court's Decision, Analysis, and Conclusion. The "Decision" section was the heart of the casenote, a section which described in detail the court's reasoning, methodology, tests, and authorities. This section would demonstrate that the student was competent. The "Analysis" section, however, was where a student could shine. In this section, we were to explain the positive and/or negative impact of the case: Is the decision consistent with prior jurisprudence? Does it make a significant advance in the law? If so, is this advance warranted or does it conflict with the goals of the particular area of law?

Pretty basic rules, although there would be the inevitable confusion. Would the footnotes have to be triple-spaced also? Would a paper failing to comply with a rule be docked points or completely disqualified?

The meeting ended with excitement in the air. People huddled around the desk at the front of the room to get a copy of the official rules. I dropped off an extra set with Tommy Wong. He'd had to miss the meeting for a doctor's appointment; he was suffering from migraines, a result of stress. Everyone I knew, it seemed, had suffered some physical manifestation of stress. Some had headaches, others had rashes, muscle tension, sleepless nights, bleeding gums. For a period that first year, the pain in my chest was so bad I was sure my heart was bursting. I would sit at my desk trying to get through the day's reading, trying to keep up with the class, trying to get ahead for once, and the burning in my chest would force me to walk around, drink water, breathe deeply. Try to relax. Shake it off. Although I knew I was basically being foolish, that my cholesterol level was good, that my heart rate was strong, that I got exercise walking back and forth to school, I still worried. I didn't know what was causing the problem. If

I didn't drop from a massive coronary, perhaps the stress would just wear down the heart's lining. Perhaps I would need a transplant or suffer a slow painful death, law school having taken years off my life.... Whatever it was, the pain disappeared after final exams. The storm in my stomach eventually passed.

Tommy would be all right. In the meantime, his doctor had given him pills that looked like they could tranquilize a horse. He held the bottle up to the light in the kitchen.

"Are you really going to try to write on?" I asked him.

"Law Review is one of those things you just have to try for," Tommy said. "It's sort of a quintessential law school experience."

We both looked at his bottle of tranquilizers. I thought he sounded pretty confident.

August 30
(Saturday)

For the rest of that first week, I concerned myself mostly with class-work. I would get started on the casenote, I figured, over the weekend. I had to get started eventually. Wasn't this what being in law school was all about? I owed at least this much to myself. At least I could make the effort. Nothing ventured, nothing gained. Eighty percent of life is just showing up.... I would at least make the effort. That was the least I could do.

During breaks in my class schedule I found myself watching with curiosity the people who had graded onto Law Review. I suppose I expected to see something special. Often I would see them standing by the elevator inside the Freret Street entrance, waiting to take the ride to their fourth floor offices. I always slowed my step as I passed, not star-ing but taking it all in, their stance, their expressions, the number of books they carried. Outside, sitting on the cement wall waiting for Katie to pick me up, I would watch their slow gait across the parking lot from the University Center to the law school, a Styrofoam container of food in one hand, a drink in the other. They would be eating lunch in the office, I figured, a habit they would continue to follow, sporadically, throughout their careers.

Visions of winning a spot on Law Review competed with the fear of falling two weeks behind in my school work. For several days, I didn't seem capable of accomplishing anything. I asked Jonathan if he was going to enter the competition. He didn't like to be a measuring stick for other people, I could tell, but he admitted that he was going to try.

"I feel like I should at least make the effort," I agreed.

"You're wasting your time if you don't give it your best shot," he told me. "You're just wasting your time."

He was right. Absolutely. I think I knew all along that I would make the effort. Now I would give it my best shot. The only excuse for not doing something is that you don't want to do it. Never give up, never give up, never, never, never give up ...

So that weekend I sat down at my desk in the kitchen and started to read the cases.

4

I decided to write my casenote on *LaFleur v. Connecticut General Life Insurance Co.*, a case concerning the Employee Retirement Income Security Act of 1974 (ERISA), a federal statute which dealt with employee benefit plans. The facts of *LaFleur* seemed to lend themselves to an interesting paper. A married man is shot by his lover. The man's widow, Mrs. LaFleur, tries to collect her husband's death benefits under his employee benefit package. The insurance company argues successfully in the lower court, primarily on the basis of the lover's testimony, that the husband instigated the attack and therefore brought about his own death, which was a sufficient basis for denying benefits.

I didn't know anything about ERISA, but the case had only three "headnotes," brief summaries of the law contained in the case. One of these headnotes, one of these rules of law, had to significantly alter the prevailing law in some respect. Of course, I would have to understand the case completely. I would have to read it numerous times, read the cases to which it referred, read cases on the same issue that had been decided since, check the law reviews and anything else I could find to better form an opinion on the merits of the case and its significance to ERISA.

September 4
(Wednesday)
(1:55 p.m.)

I stood in the hallway looking at the closed door. Through the window I could see Tommy Wong and Francis Penwell, and next to Tommy an empty seat where I should have been. How I had gotten the idea that B.E. began at two o'clock I couldn't say, but for the past hour, while I prepared for class, Tarenzella had been going on happily without me.

I shouldn't have let missing a class bother me. Early in the semester, it's easy to make that kind of mistake. Students frequently open doors, stick their heads in a classroom, and retreat just as quickly. Wrong class. Wrong day. Wrong time. Still, I felt bad. A few weeks into law school you begin to realize that if you had to read, let alone master, all of the material on a subject, there wouldn't be enough time in the day. A close look at the titles on the shelves of the library is usually persuasive. Entire rows are devoted to various courses. The more law a person reads, the more there is to read. The more details one absorbs, the more amorphous the monster becomes. The merits and scope of the law often depend on who is speaking. Each expounder on the law tries to put the material into a neat package, and each package ends up looking a little different. Some people do well without ever attending class, but they either know what the professor thinks is important or just don't care. I never seemed to know the people with the great outlines. I didn't seek them out. It didn't matter. I was going to attend class regardless. At least I would get that much for my $25,000 a year tuition.

Assuming I could keep my schedule straight.

September 5
(Thursday)

The next morning, a familiar voice stopped me in the hallway. It was Robert Calhoun, one of the students I had clerked with over the summer at Simoneaux. He was also a 2L, and I asked him about his classes.

"I'm only taking twelve hours," he told me right off. "With the writing competition and everything, I thought I'd take a lighter load, get the old grade-point up."

"You been spending a lot of time on the competition?"

He admitted he had. I imagined he was killing himself. Not grading onto Law Review had been a big disappointment. After an outstanding first semester, he had sputtered somewhat in the spring. The advantage his paralegal training had given him initially had worn thin as other students became more at ease with the language of law. Still, he remained in the top fifteen percent of the class. Pretty strong overall. But not Law Review.

I started once again to think seriously about dropping Federal Procedure. Robert was stiff competition. He had received good responses to his writing over the summer. There would be others who could express their ideas clearly, forcefully. Besides, my summer work had reduced me to a lump of ashes. Others who hadn't worked would be out to prove themselves. Interviews would in all likelihood take a fair amount of time. The Law Review competition would take an enormous amount of time. And I needed to protect my grade-point, which became perhaps the most persuasive consideration. If the fall interviews didn't produce an offer, if I was still looking for a job in the spring, my semester grades would be that much more important …

"Have you heard from Simoneaux?" I asked.

"Just about the cocktail party."

"What cocktail party?"

"Maybe I shouldn't have said anything," he said, cackling just enough to irritate me. "Barbara was here just a little bit ago passing out invitations."

"Barbara was here? When?" Barbara was the recruiting coordinator at Simoneaux.

"Just a little bit ago," he said. "There's probably one in your folder."

"Yeah." I wasn't sure.

"I wrote Simoneaux and told them I wanted to come back," he said.

"I thought you might be interested in going back to New York. Isn't that where you're from, New York?"

"Can't burn any bridges, my boy."

"Right."

I thought about the letters I had sent to Simoneaux at the close of the summer, little notes thanking various members of the firm and hoping they had found my work satisfactory. Overall, the letters had a tone that might have been interpreted as farewell. That was sort of my intention. In truth, I didn't expect to go back. I didn't expect I'd have to.

I left Robert to check my folder in the student lounge and, to my great relief, found a small cream envelope.

Simoneaux, Troy & Walters
cordially invite you to a cocktail party
at the Columns Hotel
on September 11.

Perhaps there was still a chance, I thought.

That afternoon, I dropped Federal Procedure, giving me 12 credit hours. I would make up the class later, when I had more time, fewer commitments. To celebrate, I headed off for the big brother/big sister party on the law school patio. The idea was to match 1Ls with upper-class students who would help them adjust to law school. Several days before, the name of my "little sister" had been placed in my folder: Carmen Constantine. I went to the meeting thinking she might be there, although neither of us had attempted to communicate with the other.

As it turned out, I couldn't have found her in any event. People milled about aimlessly, content with the free soft drinks and sandwiches cut into little triangles. I had a few sandwiches and left. The committee had forgotten to bring name tags.

September 6
(Friday)

In Evidence, Landrow continued to give us advice about conducting a trial: Consider how your questions will read later in the trial transcript. Avoid too many negatives. Object with a layman's explanation so the jury will understand your complaint. Make your closing direct, simple, vivid. Always phrase your questions as statements and end with, "is that correct?" Don't browbeat the witness on cross-examination. If you have nothing to accomplish on cross-examination, don't even stand up. Break your strong points into little pieces and get the witness to keep saying yes, yes, yes. And for goodness' sake, if you don't know the answer, don't ask the question.

Landrow gave us so much to think about, I could see it would be easy for the novice to make numerous tactical errors. There was so much to think about, a person could be a novice at litigation for years.

Much of the remainder of the course would concern foundation and relevance, the two basic impediments to getting evidence admitted. Proving foundation meant proving that an object is what it purports to be or that a witness has knowledge of that about which she speaks. Evidence is relevant if it makes a fact of consequence to the determination of the case more or less probable. The better the foundation, the more likely a piece of evidence is what it purports to be. The more likely a piece of evidence is what it purports to be, the more relevant it becomes. Green threads found in a trunk of a murder suspect become relevant if the victim wore a green sweater, more relevant if the thread is wool and the victim wore a green wool sweater. If the evidence is admissible, an attorney can argue all reasonable inferences therefrom, which means the attorney can convey to the jury an image of the defendant stuffing the victim's body in his trunk, an image that would be repeated over and over throughout the trial.

September 7
(Saturday)

I had begun my work on *LaFleur,* the case on which I would write my casenote, by going over it in painstaking detail. I paraphrased each paragraph until I thought I understood what the case was saying. That would be my strength, I thought. I would look at the case until the lens twisted into focus and the peculiar universe suddenly made sense.

The real issue in *LaFleur,* it turned out, was the appropriate standard of review in benefit denial cases. With this, I backed up for a broad view of the material. Using the online computer services in the library, I scanned the law reviews for anything that looked like a discussion of the standard of review or the general purposes of ERISA. I read the relevant sections of every case I could find. The passages containing the key words popped up on the screen. I must have skimmed a hundred cases in that way, trying to get a sense of ERISA. I was dealing with a statute on which I could appear incompetent with every assertion. There was much to do.

Saturday night I was sitting on the edge of the couch in my living room, working off a card table, typing into my little word processor with stacks of papers everywhere. I looked up and saw Howard Sloan, the 1L from across the hall, standing in the doorway, contemplating the scene. I had left the door ajar. We shared a common hallway, and Howard was used to letting himself in. But tonight I didn't feel like talking. I was a little embarrassed by my approach to legal problem-solving, ankle-deep in papers, books stacked on the arm of the couch, the lampshade removed so I could make out the words on my word processor. I did not like to be seen making the effort. And what an effort. Here it was, Saturday night, ten-thirty, and I was hard at work. It upped the ante for failure.

"You'd better get good grades or you'll be doing the same thing," I told him. He didn't say anything to that. He had the idea, I suppose, that he would get good grades. Everyone does their first year.

Howard wanted us to come over to his place and watch a comedy show on TV. Katie went over for a bit. I sat staring at my little computer screen. Even with the shade off the lamp I was having a hard time making out what I had written. The geniuses who designed the thing had not backlit the screen, and I sat there squinting, too poor or too stubborn to buy an upgrade.

I went to the kitchen and opened a beer just to renew some faith in myself.

Later that night, I looked out the bedroom window to see if Jonathan was home yet.

"Jonathan's light is out," I told Katie. "I don't see his car. He's probably still at the library."

"The library's closed," she said. "It's twelve-thirty."

"He left at twelve, and now he's on his way home. His car hasn't been parked out there all day."

Katie didn't respond. I waited and then watched her as she crossed the hallway to the bathroom.

September 9
(Monday)

Tarenzella was one of those professors who seemed determined to know everyone by name. Even so, I often went to B.E. unprepared. With the Law Review competition, I was falling behind in all my class work. In B.E., I don't think I ever caught up. Too much was going on. Others were taking the class lightly. I sloughed along as well, liberal arts degree and all.

Tarenzella had recently plunged into the Uniform Partnership Act. I marked sections she referred to in class, highlighting passages she thought were of particular importance. Reading statutes is much easier at the end of the semester, anyway, I figured, when the course has assumed greater shape. I would try to read it all straight through closer to exams, probably over Thanksgiving, the last chance to grapple with the material before the crunch. I would read it, study it, but would I have it on the tip of my tongue when I walked into the exam? I wasn't sure. The idea of a closed book exam continued to bother me so much so that I put a typewritten note in Tarenzella's mailbox:

> **Dear Ms. Tarenzella:**
>   **Because you have not definitively announced what students are allowed to bring with them into the exam, we would like to take this opportunity to encourage you to give an "open note" exam. A law school exam should not reward those students with the best short-term memory. Students should be rewarded for their ability to put the course together into a comprehensive whole, something which is encouraged by allowing a student to bring an outline to the final exam.**
>   **Very truly yours,**
>   **Concerned Students**

"I got your note about the exam," Tarenzella told the class the following Monday. People didn't understand. "I'm considering an open note exam," she went on, which invoked a cry of approval from several students, some clapping of hands. I had a good feeling that Tarenzella could be persuaded. I never did like rote memorization. There had to be a better use of one's time than memorizing the table of contents of the casebook. With an open note exam, if you understood the basic concepts of the course, you could make a chart where different theories or rules overlapped in interesting ways. This at least required some creativity. You could plot the course in skeletal fashion over a few pages and find a way to answer almost any question that might arise.

In class, we were discussing the concept of apparent authority, specifically whether a shipping company had to pay for hundreds of cigarette cartons purchased by the ship's captain. The answer, as always, depended on the facts. Did the captain purport to act in a representative capacity? Had the shipping company granted the captain this authority? Was purchasing cigarettes within the realm of the captain's ordinary duties? Did the shipping company make the limitations of the captain's authority known to all parties? Should the suppliers of the cigarettes have known that the captain was without authority or did they have a duty to make further inquiries?

The shipping company won, but Tarenzella did a good job showing how changing the facts slightly in various ways would alter the outcome. That was what we did, day after day, our entire first year of law school. We would do it for two years more. It was what we were being trained to do. Just change the facts slightly and a loser becomes a winner. It was called learning to think like a lawyer.

5

September 10
(Tuesday)

We were now in the final stretch of the Law Review competition. The casenotes were due Wednesday at five o'clock. No late papers accepted. I decided I couldn't spare the time to go to Pollution Control, so I sent Katie instead. When she came home, I wanted all the details. She sat at the back of the room, she said. Muder hadn't even noticed her.

"Did you see Jonathan or Tommy?"

"Both of them."

"What'd you say?"

"I explained that I was taking notes for you."

"Yeah."

"Jonathan seemed a little insulted."

"What'd he say?"

"He said to Tommy, "'I wish I had one of those.'"

"Did you tell him you were interested in Pollution Control and were interested in what Muder might say?"

"I went into all that."

We sat down and went through the notes. The class was still trying to figure out what was in the Clean Water Act and what was out. To be covered by the Act, something had to be a "point source," which was defined by the Act as "any discernible, confined and discrete conveyance." But what did these words mean? What a court would ultimately define as a point source would depend on a number of conflicting policies that judges would weigh, either explicitly or implicitly, to ascertain what the legislature likely intended. For example, if a hydroelectric dam is ultimately found to be a point source, there would be a huge rise in sewer and water bills. If shell dredging is a point source, then shell dredgers are out of business.

The approach of most courts was that the Clean Water Act didn't mean everything it said. Katie had taken down Muder's sentiments verbatim: "Somewhere along the line, zero discharge got lost."

*   *   *

I wasn't the only one working around the clock on my casenote. Stan Washington, who lived across the hall from Jonathan, admitted to putting in long hours. Jonathan's light had been on until five Sunday night and late again on Monday. I imagined him putting the final touches on his paper. That was further along than I was. When I asked about his progress, he admitted to being curious about mine as well.

"I look over sometimes to see if you're up," he said, "but I can't always tell."

"I can shut the door in the living room and leave the rest of the apartment dark," I told him.

By Tuesday, my paper was finally and furiously coming together. The Fifth Circuit in *LaFleur* had drawn a distinction between the standard of review for factual determinations and plan term interpretations. Whether Mr. LaFleur had brought about his own death, the Fifth Circuit decided, was a factual determination, and the standard of review for factual determinations should be "abuse of discretion." The prevailing Supreme Court case on the standard of review in benefit denial cases, *Firestone Tire & Rubber Co. v. Bruch*, required instead a "de novo" standard of review, which was much more favorable to an appellant. A court using this standard would give no deference to the lower court's decision.

To evaluate the merits of *LaFleur*, then, it was necessary to determine the scope of the Supreme Court decision. Did the Supreme Court intend a "de novo" standard of review for factual determinations only, as the Fifth Circuit argued, or did the Supreme Court intend the standard to apply to both factual determinations and plan term interpretations?

The solution came to me one morning over breakfast. The Fifth Circuit had needlessly clouded the issue, drawing a distinction never made by the Supreme Court. The more I read the opinion, the more it seemed that the Supreme Court, rather than making a distinction between factual determinations and plan term interpretations, was making a distinction between Section 1132(a)(1)(B) and other remedial provisions.

The lens had twisted into focus. Perhaps. The key to making out an argument that the Supreme Court's standard of review should apply to *LaFleur* still depended on finding other remedial provisions available to ERISA plaintiffs. The day before the paper was due I found what I was looking for. Searching the law review articles on remedies available under ERISA, I found a Cornell Law Review article which led me to a relevant U.S. Supreme Court case. In a strong concurring opinion, Justice Brennan argued the applicability of another ERISA section to permit the recovery of compensatory damages to plan participants. Now I had the other remedial provision necessary to make my argument, the missing piece of the puzzle. Still, it was only a concurring opinion. I needed more before I could realistically argue that the Fifth Circuit was destroying a careful scheme established by ERISA and supported by the Supreme Court.

Returning to the online computer services in search of cases citing Brennan's concurring opinion, I struck gold: a Sixth Circuit opinion credited Brennan's arguments and permitted the recovery of compensatory damages to plan participants. The picture was complete.

By providing for *de novo* review in Section 1132(a)(1)(B) actions challenging the denial of benefits based on plan interpretations, the Supreme Court effectively shifted the focus to Section 1132(a)(3). This change would make the determination of remedies under ERISA focus on whether the fiduciary had acted in the sole interest of the employee benefit plan, which critics had long argued was the best way to ensure the goals of ERISA were forcefully advanced.

It was radical, a little of a high-wire act, but I was shot full of adrenaline. I felt as if I had gotten inside the Supreme Court's collective mind, looking at a conclusion it would like to reach and finding a way to get there with the applicable law and language.

"I've said this before," I told Katie. "Two good things can happen this semester: I could make Law Review and I could get an offer from Gaines." Gaines was the law firm in Columbus that I most hoped would make me an offer of summer employment. Now journal experience seemed within my grasp, and with journal experience I did not see how Gaines could turn me away.

We were both happy.

I called my dad. He sounded like he was eating something. Popcorn, I imagined. I told him I had just called to check in, to say that the paper was going well. I blurted out my breakthrough.

He laughed. "I always thought you started with the law and drew a conclusion from that instead of the other way around."

Crazy kid.

So I spent Tuesday going through the material I had gathered over the past week, looking quickly at notations I had made, supplying footnotes to my draft. By two in the morning, I noted changes I would make the next day on the word processor, then stumbled off to bed.

September 11 (Wednesday)

The next day I was at school an hour before B.E. I went to the library and tried to read the assignment. It was slow going. I was so far behind

I had trouble understanding even the major thrust of the material. I was also beginning to worry that I wouldn't have time after class to type all my changes and make copies of the casenote by five o'clock.

I was right to worry. Making the changes on the word processor took longer than I had anticipated. The computer was no help. I had to go through the text and delete spaces every time I changed a paragraph so the lines would run across the page properly. Footnotes were being thrown in. I had no time to proofread. Katie had the car home at four-thirty, but the paper was still printing. Four minutes per page. The computer finished printing with eighteen minutes to spare, and still I had to make seven copies and get up to the third floor of the law school before the door was locked at five o'clock sharp. Why was I always working up to the last minute? Some day things would be different. Katie went down and started the car. I was right behind her. Why couldn't I just get the paper finished at a decent hour, get seven hours of sleep, and live a long and healthy life? Why?

There were two minutes to spare when I took my place in line in Wehrle's office. He was the advisor to the Law Review. I was lucky. There hadn't been a single customer at the copy center. Katie had buzzed me from the copy center to school without a hitch. At the front of the line, I handed the seven stapled copies to Wehrle's secretary. She put a sticker with the number 0062 on the front of each one. I signed my name next to that number on a sheet for her records, and she gave me a card bearing the same number. I was not to show the card to anyone.

*   *   *

The Simoneaux party was to begin at six o'clock that evening, but as I watched the national news I still hadn't decided if I would go. I was tired. The party would be draining. Somehow I rose to my feet. If there was any chance of a job offer, I had to go. If there was no chance of a job offer, I had to go. I could still eat, drink, and be merry. Hey, I could get along without Simoneaux and the rest of them.... And with the casenote behind me, I guess I deserved a party.

The party, it was immediately apparent, was not what I had expected. I had expected to see only the twenty-four clerks I had worked with at Simoneaux over the summer, but I arrived to find the hotel crawling with law students, stumbling over themselves on the front porch like brown beetles. Inside, a party was raging, with several makeshift bars and a grand buffet. Surrounding me were members of the Tulane and Loyola Law Reviews. This was a recruiting party. I saw Tabatha Parish, a 3L from Loyola and one of the clerks I'd worked with over the summer. It was no secret how much she wanted an offer from Simoneaux. I asked her how her semester was going.

"Working hard," she said. "A lot of work on MOOT COURT." She kept walking.

I found the bar. Sooner or later, everyone would come to me. Sooner or later, they did. I quickly gathered that the attorneys at Simoneaux had reason to celebrate. Earlier in the day, the firm had distributed $15 million to its members, a settlement from an anti-trust case won, for all practical purposes, when the attorneys representing the other side failed to file an appeal. Even new associates had pocketed $5,000 apiece. Everyone was jovial. Rick Lasby, the firm's king of casualty, strode across the room wearing the name tag of someone named Jeannie Trumbull.

"Hi, Jeannie," I said.

"Kenneth," he said, "I didn't recognize you with that wedding ring." He kept walking, too.

Robert Calhoun leaned over and told me, "Jeannie Trumbull is number one in her class."

"She's a Three L?"

"She could work anywhere she wants."

"Where's she going to work?"

"I think she's taken a judicial clerkship."

Robin Carey passed by and told me what a terrible mentor she had been. I'd had two mentors at Simoneaux: one a partner, the other an associate. Robin was the associate. We were supposed to become good friends. It just never happened. I shook my head, touched her shoulder. It was true that I had gotten a break when I landed the job at Simoneaux. My grades weren't as good as those of the other clerks. In fact, my first semester grades, just outside the top third of my class, were well below Simoneaux standards. Almost certainly I was taking the place of someone much better qualified. Around Robin, though, that was something I was never able to forget.

Robert Calhoun came around again later, wanting to talk about the casenote. "I suppose it's all right to talk about the contest now, isn't it?" he said. "That new Bluebook style ..." He smiled. His tongue hung on his lower set of teeth. "Did you get that? There were some big changes. The new style completely does away with parallel citations."

I must have looked thoughtful.

"Maybe we shouldn't talk about the contest," he said, cackling just enough to irritate me.

"No, I know what you're saying. I just didn't think of it like that. I hardly referred to the Bluebook at all. I went mostly from models I found in the recent volume of the Tulane Law Review. How many people do you think entered?"

"About seventy."

"That sounds right to me because I'm sixty-two and there were people behind me. They put two zeros in front of the number, but I figured they started at one. I turned the paper in a couple of minutes before five."

"I turned mine in around noon."

"I wish I could get my papers in early."

"There were only twenty-four people then," he said.

"I believe there were seventy.... Things might have been different if they hadn't told us continually how only forty people entered last year."

"How'd the paper turn out?" he asked.

"I was up all night getting the thing written."

"I wanted to turn mine in and get it over with," he said.

"I turned it in with some glaring errors."

"Oh, mine had glaring errors," he said. "Oh, man ..."

September 12
(Thursday)

When I woke the next morning, I realized I was dead. It was with a jolt that I realized I had given out the number of my casenote in a room filled with members of the Law Review. I may have said it loudly, may have even repeated it. I didn't know for sure. We were near the bar. I tried to think but had no real details to draw upon, just snippets of conversation. I knew the rules, though. The rules strictly forbade sharing our numbers with anyone. Not only had I shared my number, I had shared it in a place where I was almost certain to have been overheard by a member of the Law Review. All that time, so many evenings, two straight nights without sleep. It was all at risk. The thought was sickening.

September 13
(Friday)

This lawyer's plane crashed on a tropical island inhabited by cannibals. The lawyer went to the local deli and saw behind the glass a number of brains for sale. One sign said, "Doctor's Brain $5/lb." Another said, "Accountant's Brain $5/lb." When he saw a lawyer's brain selling for $50 a pound, he swelled with pride.

"Is that because lawyers are so smart?" he asked the butcher.

"No," the butcher told him. "It just takes more lawyers to get a pound."

In Evidence class, we were discussing the subject of relevance. Landrow was explaining that, to be relevant, evidence must make a fact of consequence to the determination of the outcome more or less probable than without the evidence. The problem was that relevant evidence could at times have a prejudicial impact. That a robbery suspect has committed fifteen other robberies is relevant, but the evidence is kept out because it would be prejudicial and confusing. The suspect is not being tried for those other crimes. The general rule, then, was that relevant evidence is admissible unless it is substantially outweighed by the prejudicial impact.

September 17
(Tuesday)

Muder began class by showing us articles from the morning newspaper that had to do with the environment. The EPA had issued new landfill regulations, American Indians had adopted state standards for controversial waste projects, and Australia was considering plans for a major landfill. Environmental issues did seem to occupy a great deal of the media's attention.

Today we would begin to put together the Clean Water Act in a meaningful way. Muder, admitting that she was speaking "alphabet soup," flew from one section to another to another while we paged back and forth in the statute. I was furiously taking down what notes I could. Everyone was struggling to write down what Muder said. This was the blood and guts of the statute. We needed to get every word.... In Pollution Control, there was always a beat after Muder finished her lecture before people began to pack up their books. After she finished showing us how the various provisions of the CWA fit together, four beats passed. Was it over? Was she finished? Like others, I knew that we were just getting started. I heard a fellow behind me say, "This outline is going to be a bear." I couldn't begin to conceive putting this patchwork into outline form. I was sure, though, that a traditional outline would be of little use.

*   *   *

By a stroke of luck, the Environmental Law Journal announced that it would consider for its "write on" competition casenotes that were acceptable in the Law Review competition. Over the course of a week, I polished up my casenote. Surely I would still be in the running for the ELJ, as it was called. I had done nothing to violate its rules. I hadn't threatened the integrity of the contest one jot. Any disqualification would be punishment unbefitting the crime. I would file a complaint with the school. I would hire the best criminal defense lawyer in New Orleans. We would show up and blow those little twerps on the Ethics Committee out of the water.

The day the casenote was due, I sat in Remedies class listening to Worth discuss preliminary and permanent injunctions. When is it wrong to enjoin misconduct without clear indication the defendant will repeat the conduct? And there was Worth, standing in front of us, looking off over our heads as if the answer were written on the windows, as if there were some response for the poor sap whose neighbor built his house two feet over the property line.

At four o'clock, I made my way to the loading dock to meet Katie, but she was not there. Still making copies of the ELJ casenote, I figured. The paper was due at four o'clock. I still had forty minutes. The revisions had gone well. The paper had been finished the night before. Everything, I thought, was going along smoothly, but Katie still hadn't arrived, and it would be another thirty minutes before she ran across the lawn of the law school explaining that the car had run out of gas, that she had thought she would make it, that the car was safe—we could get it later—and, no, she had not yet made copies of the casenote.

We would have to use the copy machines in the library. Ten minutes was plenty of time. We would be okay as long as everyone else hadn't waited until the last minute, as long as a legal research and writing project wasn't due, as long as a little luck was on our side.

"Did you read it?" I asked Katie.

"It's good," she said.

"You read it?"

"I started it. The first paragraph reads very good. Professional. I was proud."

We found an empty copy machine. Only one other person appeared to be copying a casenote. She wasn't paying any attention to us. I made the copies. Katie sorted. The ELJ required five copies. Katie had brought along a stapler. We put the package together and ran down to the records office where the casenotes were being collected.

"Do you have an index card?" the secretary asked when I handed her my work.

"No …" I had forgotten to bring a five-by-seven index card for my name and social security number.

"I have one here," she said.

Someone had been kind enough to leave some extras with her. I quickly wrote my name and social security number on the card and added my papers to a very high stack.

6

These days, just getting accepted into law school is an achievement. Everyone, it seems, wants to be a lawyer. In 1965, one in every 695 people were lawyers. By 1988, the figure was one in 340. There are almost as many people in law school today as there are lawyers. In the near future there will be more than one million lawyers. Applications at Tulane increased more than fifty percent in the 1990s, up to about 2,800 for approximately 325 positions. Nearly 150,000 people jostle to be one of the 43,000 students who begin law school each year. Being accepted to law school is the only career goal many have had their entire adult lives, the culmination of four or five years of pretty serious studying, years spent with their grade-point averages clutched between their teeth like a bit and always the sound of the reins in their ears. *Law school.* The words have an emotional appeal, an image, a color. *I'm going to law school.* It's an achievement and sometimes a surprise to get into a particular law school. *I'm going to Tulane Law School.* The entire process and the sense of accomplishment tend to brainwash students into thinking they are about to embark upon the hardest course of study imaginable. They're told numerous times they're now average among the exceptional. They start to believe it. Why shouldn't they? They've seen the movies. They've read the books. But the work they set for themselves is endless, the hours impossible, and others always seem to work harder, read faster, do better in class. They panic, often before the work really gets underway.

The fear of law school stems in large part from the sheer amount of reading material. The stack of casebooks, statutes, hornbooks, and outlines purchased at the beginning of the semester will likely reach several feet high. Didn't a character in *One L* click his heels and head off to the library to read his way through law school? What else were all those books for? Wasn't wisdom to be found in the shelves upon shelves of clay-colored tomes? Wasn't the number of books in the library key criteria in the law school's ranking? In a world where success is based upon the curve, where getting ahead of someone else is the name of the game, the library is the place to set up shop.

So when it came time to get back to studying, to start to catch up with my reading, I naturally headed off to the library. It was a place I already knew quite well. As a 1L, all of my spare time, it seemed, was spent in a cold plastic chair at a metal desk beneath a buzzing light with a yellowed cord. It was a place with crude comments on the walls and the odd occasional smell of glue.

Most of the desks in the belly of the law school library were assigned to members of Moot Court, Law Review, Environmental Law Journal, Maritime Law Journal, International Law Journal, Journal of Law and Sexuality, graduate students, research assistants, and the like. Some of the stalls looked as if they had been occupied for years. Books of all sorts and papers were stacked pell-mell. There were coffee makers, open briefcases, seat cushions, jackets on the wall, pictures of family and friends, softball gloves, fans, electric pencil sharpeners, magazines, newspapers, toilet paper, toothbrushes, dirty socks.... These were little living rooms, locker rooms, studies. Some stalls, no matter how cluttered or what time of day, never seemed to be occupied. Others almost always had someone crouched there, neck bent. The stalls most hidden in the building, on the lower floors, were the most likely to be occupied at any given time. Down there, I noticed, the people might as well have been speaking a different language. They laughed loudly at things that made little sense.

My favorite desk was on the second floor. Although the desk supposedly belonged to a research assistant—her name was on a piece of paper taped to the wall—nothing else on the desk indicated possession, not so much as a candy wrapper. So I took up residence and quickly became aware of those nearby.

The fellow who sat at the desk around the corner from me turned out to be sort of a legal guru. At first, the sound of people talking to him every time I sat down almost forced me to move. Gradually, I began to listen to what they said. The talk, it seemed, took on a general pattern. After some introductory remarks by the passer-by, a particular question would be posed. What do you think? Then the legal guru would carefully explain some aspect of the law. There was no stammering or uncertainty. He never flipped through his casebook. He just gave the answer. Few follow-up questions were needed. Whoever asked the question was usually too embarrassed to ask for more. There would be an expression of gratitude, although the voice sometimes seemed more shaken than comforted, followed by a shuffling of feet down the hall.

After I began to take note of the legal guru, it seemed to me as if he were always in the library, always at his table. I would walk through at nine in the morning, and he would be sitting there, legs casually crossed, slowing turning the pages of the *New York Times*. On my way out, he would be marking his casebook with slow straight lines or writing an outline in a spiral notebook with the same deliberate care. He occasionally looked up as I passed as if he expected me to stop. I got the idea he was one of those who treated law school like a job. That was advice we had been given as 1Ls: Treat law school like a job. If you're smart enough to be accepted to law school, you're smart enough to learn the law. Sitting down and working eight or ten hours a day is a sure way to do it. This fellow had the patience, the brains, the desire. He would never stay up all night cramming for an exam. He would get mostly A's. His professors would like him and his fellow students would admire him. He knew that learning the law was not something to be rushed. He was a fisher of wisdom, content to sit on the bank, day after day, basking in the sunshine of the law and catching all that came his way.

Different people find different things to love about the law. Scott Turow loved the fact that knowledge of the law amplified his understanding of the routines of daily life. Louis Auchincloss loved the tight prose of carefully written judicial opinions. Others enjoyed the search for meaning, the idea of learning, the self-respect learning can bring. And some sat all day reading in a damp, cramped library with low ceilings and bad lighting and saw themselves behind powerful desks making powerful decisions. When these people graduate and take jobs with large firms, they don't care that their desks face away from the view of the city; they have the world at their feet.

My study routine the first year consisted of reading the cases for class the night before, underlining the facts and issues in black, the losing argument in blue, the winning argument in red, and the reasons for the decision—or "holding"—in green. Before class I would go over the case again in the library, taking notes and making sure I had a general idea of the facts and outcome and significance. Fear of performing poorly in class is a powerful motivator. That fear dissipated dramatically the second year. Professors were more content to lecture, students more comfortable saying they weren't prepared. Often, students knew in advance who would be called to speak on a particular day, and those not designated "experts" had little reason to agonize over fact patterns as common as lightening strikes or to spend hours on the nuances of rules that hadn't been the law for decades.

Because Tarenzella was one of those professors who expected us to be prepared, who often called on students to state the facts of the case,

I tried to establish a routine to catch up in B.E. Even when I found, to my complete surprise, that I had gone to school on a holiday, Yom Kippur, even when every bone in my body screamed to take a much needed break, I stayed in the library to work. The treadmill had stopped but my legs continued to move mechanically. The sound of a march played in my head. I had to keep walking. I had an afternoon to make up some ground.

In this way, I dug into the study of the legal consequences of dissolving a partnership. At six o'clock, I gathered up my books and headed upstairs. The copy room was locked. So were the doors leading to the front desk. I looked through the window at my route to the outside world. The lights at the front desk were out. The librarian was gone. Everyone was gone. Everyone but me. That buzzing I had heard around five o'clock had been a signal to leave. I had thought it was a fire drill and disregarded it. Don't people walk through the library and let you know it is about to close? Shouldn't something like this be common knowledge? No one walked through. No one told me I would be locked in. No one said the least little thing.

I went to the first floor and looked at the windows. They were padlocked. It would be possible, if I were desperate enough, to throw something through the glass and jump, but I never seriously considered that option. My only concern was to find a window where I might attract Katie's attention when she came to pick me up at seven. I would have to be at the window then. And I would have to catch her before she turned the car around and pulled up to the loading dock.

In the meantime, I decided to roam around. On the first floor I found some large theatre EXIT lights I hadn't noticed before. I followed them down a short hallway to a fire exit. A striped bar stretched across the door like the arm at a railroad crossing. A large red sign warned that if the door were opened ALARM WILL SOUND. Well, I had a way out at least. If Katie didn't see me standing in the window screaming, I would break out of the library in a blaze, fire alarms sounding, sprinklers going off over my head. I got down on my hands and knees and tried to look underneath the door. I wanted a sense of where I was in the building. As well as I had come to know the law school and the library over the past year, I couldn't figure out what was on the other side of the door.

I wandered over to the reading room, strangely quiet now. This was the most inviting room in the library. The floor was carpeted, the tables large, the chairs cushioned. The room even had several sofas. Others always seemed to be sitting around the tables or sleeping in the sofas or chairs. It was nice to have the room to myself.

On one of the tables was a copy of the Environmental Law Journal that had been distributed at the beginning of the year. It was a good-looking journal, its cover forest green with a pelican etched in white across the top, the table of contents down the front a reflection of the scholarship inside. It was something to show, something to hold with care and to display with reverence. I first noticed the ELJ only a couple of weeks before when new members took turns sitting at a table in the main lobby passing them out. One member had stacked them on the desk in a spiral design, and he straightened the angles whenever someone took a copy. I had looked through the journal frequently during the competition for inspiration. This copy didn't look like it circulated. Probably someone had left it there, so I stuck it in my bookbag with my casebooks and my notes. If I joined the ELJ I would need copies to send to my father, to potential employers. I would need extra copies to start my library. Someday I would have them bound; the volumes would line a shelf behind my desk. And I sank into a comfortable chair, alone in the library, and very safe.

I was considering a little nap when my eye caught sight of a set of old books on the bottom of a nearby shelf, a collection, it turned out, of the world's great literary works. That was what I would do: I would spend the night reading Melville. After all, this was a library where Faulkner had spent time writing. I picked a volume at random, opened to Henry David Thoreau's *Walden*, and read these words:

> I have no doubt that some of you who read this book are unable to pay for all the dinners which you have actually eaten, or for the coats and shoes which are fast wearing or are already worn out, and have come to this page to spend borrowed or stolen time, robbing your creditors of an hour. It is very evident what mean and sneaking lives many of you live ... always on the limits, trying to get into business and trying to get out of debt, a very ancient slough ... always promising to pay, promising to pay, to-morrow, and dying to-day, insolvent; seeking to curry favor, to get custom, by how many modes, only not state-prison offences; lying, flattering, voting, contracting yourselves into a nutshell of civility, or dilating into an atmosphere of thin and vaporous generosity, that you may persuade your neighbor to let you make his shoes, or his hat, or his coat, or his carriage, or import his groceries for him; making yourself sick, that you may lay up something against a sick day, something to be tucked away in an old chest, or in a stocking behind the plastering, or, more safely, in the brick bank ...

*   *   *

The letter I had been expecting from Folger, Hawkins finally arrived. Folger was one of the Columbus firms I had interviewed with before the start of the semester, the firm whose hiring strategy, a young associate told me, resembled the National Football League draft: they recruited the best talent available, sure they could find a spot in their lineup. Now I learned I hadn't made the cut:

Dear Mr. Westphal:

Thank you for taking time to stop in to meet with Andy Hewett and Ollie Volgorad in my absence and for your subsequent letter concerning the meeting.

Our Hiring Committee is beginning its task in earnest of trying to determine from literally hundreds of resumes we have already received and from numerous interviews we have had on law school campuses whom we will invite for full day interviews at the firm. At this point we have reluctantly concluded that, despite your fine academic record at Ohio State and at Tulane Law School, we are not in a position to invite you back for additional interviews.

Our decision is not intended to be a negative reflection on your qualifications. Rather, it is a result of our having the good fortune of being contacted by a number of highly qualified students.

I sincerely appreciate your interest in our firm, and I wish you luck in your second year at Tulane.

Very truly yours,

Phillip C. Korovin
Hiring Committee Chair

PCK:bjs

Good news followed bad, though. Career Services notified me that I had been granted an interview with a firm in Metairie, a suburb of New Orleans. With that, the on-campus interview season was underway. At least once a week for the next several weeks I drove down to The Avenue Hotel, where the interviews were conducted, and tried to make smalltalk with lawyers about their firm's future and my own possible place therein. *Why did you leave academia? What kind of law do you want to practice? Why Tulane? What do you think of New*

Orleans? Are you interested in staying? Why our firm? Do you have any questions?... Over the next couple of weeks, I would interview with some of the larger firms in New Orleans. I read the firm resumes, studied the biographies of the attorneys, even made sure I knew the firms' representative clients, but I wasn't distinguishing myself in any way. I hadn't been able to establish instant rapport, hadn't been able to convey with certainty that I was cut of the same cloth as my interviewers.

The closest I came in those early weeks was with the firm Malone, Swope, Christy, Calumet & Franks, where I found an interviewer, a graduate of Tulane Law School, who had come to New Orleans from Indiana. What rapport we established by our mutual desire to flee mid-western winters was destroyed when, with little encouragement, I began to talk about my interest in environmental law, rambled on about how I had written a casenote for the fall contest and expected to soon become a member of the ELJ myself.

"What was your casenote about?" the environmental lawyer of the bunch wanted to know.

"Well … actually it was about ERISA."

It was like a snowstorm blew through the room. The woman from Indiana seemed to shudder. We went on talking, but well before my time was up the eldest and best dressed of the attorneys looked at his watch and then over his shoulder at the legal recruiter. He tried to catch her attention with a shake of the wrist.

The interviews all seemed to go along like that, some smoother than others, but it was like I was in an old car and felt every bump of the road.

September 25
(Wednesday)

The interview with the Kerber Wright firm would be different. I had a plan. The lawyer who had argued *LaFleur* before the Fifth Circuit Court, April Newton, worked for Kerber. If I could just show her my casenote, I thought, I'd have a decent chance of a job offer. No, this wasn't going to be just another interview; this was going to be a conversation, a meeting of minds. We were going to discuss legal theory in practice. What other recruit could do that? I read through my casenote one more time, making minor changes, and brought a copy with me to the interview. If I could just pass it along, April Newton might put in a good word for me with the Hiring Committee, I might get an invitation to the firm. I might get to meet her. She might be interested in taking me under her wing.

The two people who interviewed me had been with Kerber for six and eight years, respectively. The woman had returned to law school several years after receiving her undergraduate degree, working for a Texas firm for a year before joining Kerber. I defused questions about my out-of-state roots by asking if she was a lateral hire. She admitted that she had followed her husband to New Orleans.

"You studied English," she said. "Why did you leave?" She looked at the man as if to say: Why would anyone want to give up reading novels all day for this?

"I enjoyed it," I said. "It was something I wanted to do. I had the chance to teach."

"Oh, you taught," she said, looking again at my resume.

"I taught English composition at Ohio State for three years." I went into a little soliloquy about graduate school, a speech now quite practiced: the challenge of keeping the attention of eighteen-year-olds, my own work in rhetoric and composition under one of the giants in the field. It was a background I knew would serve me well, I enjoyed it, but I always knew I'd eventually be a lawyer.

"Are you interested in First Amendment law?" she asked.

"Does your firm do much First Amendment law?"

"Not really," she admitted. "We used to have the *Times-Picayune* for a client."

I just nodded.

"What can we tell you about our firm?" she wondered.

Now I had my chance. "I have a writing sample I'd like to leave you," I told her. "It's a casenote on *LaFleur*, a case April Newton argued before the Fifth Circuit. I thought perhaps you could pass it along."

The woman looked at the man. She looked stunned. "No one's brought this up before," she said to him before turning back to me. "I guess I should just tell you. April Newton is no longer with the firm. She left Friday."

Friday!

"Who handles the ERISA cases?" I asked.

They looked at each other and mentioned a name or two. They weren't sure. The woman rebounded: "Oh, we have some very good ERISA lawyers," she said. "You might want to send your casenote to April, anyway. I'm sure she'd love to see a casenote on her case. She's a marvelous woman."

The door was open. We were shaking hands. The room across the hall was noisy. The television blared. Children squealed. The woman thanked me very much for coming, promised to get back with me soon.

"I'm glad to have met you," I said. "Yesterday, when I was interviewing I took a wrong turn and was grilled for twenty minutes by tourists."

The woman burst out laughing.

The man smiled.

It was almost the perfect interview.

Almost.

September 26
(Thursday)

Remedies class grinded on with Professor Worth delivering his three typewritten pages of lecture notes three days a week to a class that had dwindled to a core of about fifteen students. Even the Law Review guy who sat in front of me was now missing class frequently. When he returned after a stretch, Worth admitted in an odd soliloquy that "this stuff is really pretty basic." Then Worth marched us through his prepared material, his questions spiraling forth with a blaze of ambiguity and detachment.

Jose Cadicamo was rarely attending class, and his absences were starting to concern me. When I missed class earlier in the semester, Jose had loaned me his notes. Now, the more days Jose missed, the more of my notes I figured I'd have to pass along in return. I didn't like the idea of being used to his advantage. While I went to class and worried about looking stupid, Jose was at work making money, gaining legal experience, getting something to add to his resume. When Jose did come to class, he was usually late, striding into the room, the lapels of his suit flapping lightly at his sides. He always glanced toward the podium as he entered and took his seat behind me with a comment and a chuckle. Worth went on without notice.

I wasn't comfortable with the line of cases we had been reading on reparative and structural injunctions. For a couple of days, I'd been trying to find a few hours to sit down and put some pieces together. One night after dinner, I finally worked my way through the cases, taking notes as I went along, making diagrams of the major arguments. I had four pages of notes. Then I read through my notes. I hoped something would click. With reparative injunctions, we faced the same question we had been asking all semester: What is the plaintiff's rightful position? In *Bell v. Southwell*, for example, a county commissioner had won the election but also intimidated a number of minorities from voting. Two years later, the case finally came to court. The county commissioner argued that even if all of the minorities had voted against him, he would still have won the election. The argument failed. The court sought to protect the process, not the result, and it enjoined the commissioner from serving the remaining two years of his term. But what of acts during the two years in office? How much should be undone? The questions boiled down to how much of the plaintiff's harm resulted from the defendant's wrongdoing, a question much like proximate cause, which we had wrestled with in torts the year before. Where does legal causation stop? The answer isn't in physics but rather in human judgment. It's what law professors call a policy question.

Structural injunctions were different. Here, we encountered what the casebook called the two traditions of equity. Again, the basic question was the same: What is the plaintiff's rightful position? The narrow view was that the rightful position is determined by the defendant's wrong. The wrong we were dealing with in class was deliberate school segregation. The broader view seemed first to determine the rightful position and then to work backward to the result it wanted to reach. By this logic, almost anything a court ordered that tended to bring about the rightful position was appropriate: busing, redistricting, magnet schools …

*   *   *

In Pollution Control, Muder continued to crunch the Clean Water Act into little pieces under the heel of her shoe. The CWA, she was letting us know, is a watered-down statute in a world where dilution is an unacceptable means of pollution prevention. Executive Order 12291 had mandated all agency regulations go through the Office of Management and Budget for review. To receive OMB clearance, the benefits of an agency regulation had to exceed the costs. Although Congress had said that cost was only one factor to be considered when the EPA established water regulations, the president said that costs must control. Which branch of our government runs the agency, the legislative or the executive? It was a conflict Muder built up with as much drama as she could muster.

"What is the EPA?" she asked. "Where is it in the Constitution? It acts like the legislative, judicial, and the executive branches." The EPA was supposed to give the cost of pollution control to industry merely a mild glance when it determined the best available technology required under the Clean Water Act, but once costs entered the equation, they quickly became the controlling factor. The EPA buckled. The weakness of the EPA, according to Muder, was one of the reasons the Clean Water Act didn't live up to its high expectations.

So what branch of government controls the EPA?

"It's one of the great unlitigated issues," Muder said.

But who had the final say on the Clean Water Act? students wanted to know.

Muder shrugged. "EPA figures costs when it makes regulations," she said.

September 30
(Monday)

Kerber Wright, April Newton's old law firm, didn't waste any time in responding:

> Dear Mr. Westphal:
>
> Our attorneys enjoyed meeting with you when they recently visited Tulane Law School, and your interest in Kerber Wright is appreciated.
>
> We interview many outstanding candidates for a limited number of positions in our summer program. Despite your impressive credentials, we are unable to offer a position to you at this time.
>
> Again, thank you for your interest in the Firm and for giving us the opportunity to meet with you.
> Sincerely,
>
> Robert U. Tinker
Hiring Partner

9365m

As if virtual strangers weren't giving me enough grief, I was also getting news about the drought in the legal market from friends and relatives. The year was marked by a media blitz on how bad things were in the job market in general and for lawyers in particular. And most of the major articles found their way into my mailbox. Dad sent articles from the *National Law Journal* and *Business Week. Business Week* ran the familiar graph of the bar's "swelling ranks." Ray Sharp, a neighbor of mine growing up, sent an article he had clipped from the local business daily. The headline was a real day brightener: "Law firms recruit fewer students, but quality up." It was the same old song: firms were visiting fewer campuses and law schools were reporting record numbers of applicants. The two Columbus law schools were bursting. Ohio State University's College of Law had received a record high number of applicants. Capital University was experiencing the upsurge as well. In the middle of the article I discovered why my friend Ray had sent it along. The article quoted Gwen Hollings, one of the lawyers on the Hiring Committee at Gaines, Duncan, Duffy & Gray, still the best shot I had of landing a job in Ohio. Gaines was visiting only 12 law schools this year, Gwen was quoted as saying, down from 18 the year before. Other firms were doing likewise. The number of clerks hired would be down. Although demand was still high for the best and brightest, the competition among those in the middle of the class would be fierce. It was the same old song, a terrible dirty little song I couldn't shake, that kept playing over and over in my head. *Oh to be swimmin' with bowlegged women ...*

I had been thinking of Ray Sharp lately, anyway. At times, when I seemed to grasp a point particularly quickly in B.E., it occurred to me that Ray and I had spent our childhood playing board games such as Stocks & Bonds, Mergers & Acquisitions, Tycoon. Ray had since started his own business and was doing well importing replacement casters and selling them mail order to office furniture stores across the country. Perhaps I could learn a thing or two that would be of use to him. Were there ways for him to structure his business differently? What were some of the tax consequences of the partnership? I could at least tell him with a knowing nod, "When in doubt, don't incorporate."

It would only be advice. From what I could see, the old adage that one shouldn't go into business with friends or relatives seemed to be confirmed by the number of cases we read where brother sued brother, long-time friend sued long-time friend. It was sad and ugly and real. Two friends start a business. They thrive. Ten years later they can't even speak to one another. Brothers are hiring the best lawyers they can to screw the other to the wall. The lawsuits often don't even make economic sense. The business is destroyed. Lives are wasted ...

* * *

The end of September is when Tulane's tuition comes due. I had let the bill sit on my desk for weeks. For fall semester alone I owed $12,144, which included tuition, student health insurance, and the student recreation center fee. I would graduate owing almost $75,000. In my debt, I was not alone. Seventy-five percent of my class, those who had to borrow to finance their education, owed on average in excess of $68,000. The class of 2000 would graduate with an educational debt in excess of ten million dollars.

With tuition and fees closing in on $25,000 a year, Tulane was one of the more expensive law schools in the country. And Dean Gottlieb knew more than most the toll such fees can take on students. In his article, "Paying for Law School," first published in the early 1980s when the average tuition of a private law school was half what it is today, Dean Gottlieb estimated that three years of law school, including room and board and opportunity costs, had a price tag of about $59,000, although he acknowledged that for quite a few it was much more. Debt manageability for most students, he concluded, even with debt financing, was "marginal."

Using Tulane's projected costs for 1999-2000 as a model, the cost of a private law school education today looks something like the following:

Tuition and fees for three years	$ 72,864
Room & board, health, miscellaneous	$ 35,160
Lost opportunity costs for three years	$105,000
Total	$213,024

The figures can make a person's mouth dry. If loans are taken to finance the education, the interest of ten or twenty or thirty years is also a cost to consider. Today, the cost of attending a private law school is roughly eight times as high as it was thirty years ago when Scott Turow paid $3,000 a year to attend Harvard. Starting salaries for all but a few have struggled to keep pace. The fact that one professor teaches up to 140 students at a time is supposed to make law school reasonably accessible, but today tuition is more likely to be set as high as the market will bear.

One criticism of the high cost of law school is that graduates burdened by debt can't afford to take jobs in the public interest. A number of schools have responded to this criticism by offering qualified graduates loan forgiveness programs. In 1988, Tulane became the fifteenth law school in the country to offer such a program. To be eligible, a graduate has to earn less than the starting salary for a federal lawyer and work full-time as an attorney in a private non-profit public interest organization, government agency, or private law firm for which at least 50 percent of the "billable hours" are devoted to work for persons or organizations financially unable to obtain adequate legal services. If the qualifications are met, eligible graduates pay only six percent of their disposable income toward educational debt. Tulane pays the rest, funding the program from the tuition of present students.

It is a hard subject to talk about, debt, and only rarely does it come up in conversation among students. Occasionally, someone will mumble something about borrowing $30,000 a year, usually with a wry smile. Below the surface, though, there is an anger, a frustrated anger that will spend years looking for someone to blame. But those who go to the most prestigious and expensive school they get into have no one to blame but themselves. They have already lost to their enemy. They will leave school with a degree and debt and the chance to get going, get even, get ahead. They will find themselves telling clients they certainly do not want to run up legal bills, and they will say it so often they almost believe it themselves.

Last year, the subject of debt came up most often with Tommy Wong. "You guys don't know," he would say, "I've got a wife and house payments." I had some sympathy for him, but it was hard to yield entirely. He had money in the bank. His wife was working. He wasn't taking the loans Katie and I were. From where I stood, my situation looked worse than his.

But still there was Dean Gottlieb's orientation speech rallying the students: Law is big business.... It's a multi-billion dollar a year industry. There are billions of dollars to be made providing legal services.... And we all sat there thinking, if there's so much money out there, surely I can have $50,000 of it each year. After all, that was what Tulane graduates made, on average, or at least close to that, at least if you were male and went to work for a law firm and graduated in the top third of your class. That was what was printed in Tulane's admissions bulletin. That was what we all understood from the bar graphs and the breakdowns we had been shown. And during orientation, that was what we were asked to disregard at a peculiar ceremony where we all signed a document that seemed to absolve the law school from any and all such representations.

But not to worry, Dean Gottlieb told us, we would at least pass. He didn't promise we'd all be lawyers by the end of the three years or even that we'd all think like lawyers, but he did imply that we would graduate. Very few people fail out of Tulane. "Look to your left," he told us at orientation. "Look to your right.... By the end of three years you will have *slept* with one of these people."

Yes, we would all get our degrees, as long as we paid our bills. The teaching of law, you see, is also a billion-dollar business, but we all sat there with too many dollar signs in our eyes to see there was something perverse in spending so much money to learn how to practice law from people who didn't want to practice law and that we weren't really learning how to practice law at all but learning how to "think like a lawyer" and the bar review course would teach us the law if we paid them six hundred or sixteen hundred dollars and our employers would teach us how to practice law if we could find someone who would pay us for the privilege while we learned ...

My parents tried to send some money each month. Katie's parents took over her car payments. I decided I lived better when I was delivering newspapers. At least then I could afford to buy records, see concerts, go out with friends. We were spending a fortune on education, a fortune, and our choices were being limited more each day. I told Katie I thought I could live on milk, peanut butter, lettuce, and orange juice. We frequently ate tuna casserole. We tore up the house one day searching for a missing $20 check.

"It's depressing," I told my mom. "We're spending all our wedding money on law school."

"Just think of it as an investment in your future," she said.

Yeah.

I felt bad about bringing up the subject at all. She was absolutely right. I was investing in my future.

That's what Dean Gottlieb would say. A master with facts and figures, the dean had recently begun to put numbers on the blackboard to convince us we were getting our money's worth. "Eighty thousand in loans," he told us, "consolidated, you pay $800 a month. The average legal job pays $40,000, *if you get a job*, but the average at Tulane is a little higher. From this you subtract $10,000 in state and federal taxes. I sat down and did the math myself. That's $30,000, paying $800 a month, that's $9,000, which leaves you with $21,000 in your pocket after debt and taxes, and in three-and-a-half to five years, the debt is paid off.... That's not bad. Can you buy a Mercedes? No. Can you buy a new car. Maybe. People worry about their debt, but you'll all do fine. You'll all be Yuppies."

We'll pay $1000 a month for the next fifteen or twenty years to get out from under the yoke. A few will get rich. A few will become very rich. The rest will muddle through, looking up at their classmates who did well, who went with the big firms, who joined the imperial class, the dream that keeps the rest of us in shackles.

October 4
(Friday)

As a 1L, I had told Katie on numerous occasions that things would be different the second year, once I got the hang of law school. I would know how to study more efficiently. I would know what to study.... But so far, things hadn't been much different. I was working as much as ever.

Then one day we discovered that it was Friday. We were in New Orleans. The sun never shone so bright. No casenote to write. Nothing to prevent me from making good on one of my promises. We could be in Destin, Florida, before sunfall.

"Do you want to skip your three o'clock class?" I asked. She liked that idea. I changed my mind. "No, you should go. You can't miss class. I'll pick you up at four and we're out of here."

"I can get notes," she said.

"But it's so important to go to class."

I dropped her off at Loyola and was three blocks away when the idea didn't seem so good to me, either. I turned the car around. If I hurried, I could catch her before her class started. But I had to hurry. I found a parking space half a block from the school and ran. I would check the lounge first, then the library. If she had already gone to class, she would be almost impossible to find. In that case, I'd have to come back at four. We'd get to Florida, but something would be lost along the way. So I ran up the steps of the school. I was lucky; I found her in the first place I looked, the lounge. She looked up from her casebook with an expression of complete surprise.

Outside, we could almost smell the salt air. We put on brightly colored clothes and sunglasses. We didn't even think about assignments for two days. We walked along one of the most beautiful beaches in the world, watched fishermen feed their catch to cranes, and took photographs of everything. We found a seafood festival and ate shrimp etouffee and seafood gumbo out of paper bowls. We entered a drawing to win a 1972 red Mustang convertible. We drank beer at a bar on the beach in Pensacola where the men had long hair and the women had tight jeans and everyone smoked cigarettes.

7

October 7
(Monday)

This young lawyer dies and goes to heaven. St. Peter meets him at the Pearly Gates, but when the young lawyer gives his name a suspicious St. Peter refuses to admit him. "You can't be who you say you are," St. Peter says. "You're much too young." When the young lawyer persists, St. Peter becomes adamant: "That just can't be correct, young man. I have your time sheets here, and according to the hours you've billed you should be a much older man."

The class didn't respond well, but Landrow enjoyed his joke. I was amused, but I had worked at a law firm over the summer. I knew a little about double billing, about the quarter-hour minimum, about using the telephone for fun and profit ...

In class, we were discussing three obstacles to getting a document into evidence: authenticity, hearsay, and the "best evidence rule." Generally speaking, the best evidence rule requires that the original be used to prove the content of a writing, recording, or photograph. Students often stumble over the best evidence rule, as with so many of the finer points of evidence. Landrow admitted that even he had misunderstood the rule early in his teaching career. While ordinarily the written account must be presented, if available, when the issue involves the content of the written account, the rule doesn't prevent testimony which is otherwise admissible merely because there happens to exist a written account as well.

After class, Jonathan asked me if I had seen the Law Review notice in the hallway. I hadn't.

"Tommy made it," he said.

"One of us made it?" I said.

"Yup."

"Anyone else we know?"

"Only one other Two L. The rest were Three Ls."

"Does Tommy know?"

"He found out Friday. They called him."

Later that day, as I sat in class before the start of B.E., I watched Tommy take the long walk across the front of the classroom. He looked seven feet tall. He surveyed the room for faces. When he sat down, I told him I thought I could hear "Hail to the Chief" strike up as he entered. He shook his head; he didn't like to hear such talk.

Tommy gave me a copy of his casenote—he had also written on *LaFleur*—and reading it that night made me feel better about my chances on the ELJ. I had hit all of the basic points. I would have had a good chance at the Law Review if I had finished the paper sooner. Still, I had to admit that Tommy's paper was a fine example of how one goes about writing onto Law Review. It was competent in every way. The sentences were short. The language was clear. The footnotes followed proper form. Throughout, the paper had been proofread with care. The conclusion borrowed an argument made by another writer, but it was all carefully cited and nicely presented. Tommy's most clever trick was to use the pronoun "she" on one occasion. It gave the impression the paper had been written by a woman.

*   *   *

Muder stood before us waving a piece of paper.

"What is BAT?" she asked. BAT stood for "best available technology," which was the level of pollution control expected of industry groups. Best Available Technology. BAT. It sounded stringent, but for the past few classes we had been discussing "the funny things that can happen on the way to BAT." The EPA, because of cost considerations, had watered down the technological requirements from the "best available" to the "best practicable." In one case, the EPA rejected stringent pollution controls for the disposal of fish parts because the controls were "not adequately demonstrated," although the technology in question was used by 25 percent of the industry.

"It should have been BAT," Muder said, "and the EPA was arguing it wasn't even practicable."

Today, Muder had another point to make. "Does BAT allow for brown paper?" she asked. "Does paper have to be white? Are there other ways to make fertilizer? Are these other ways even considered? What is BAT? Does BAT accept every fool thing that makes money? Making paper or using chlorine to make paper? Should we require paper manufacturers to face a zero dioxin standard? What is the scope of the inquiry? What is the purpose of the industry inquiry? What is the best available technology?" These were rhetorical questions. We all sat spellbound. "What BAT really tries to do is to make it so difficult to discharge that companies face cost barriers. But Congress is careful not to move into industrial decision-making. It takes a rather indirect approach. It stops pollution at the discharge pipe ..." She shook her head. "It's like changing a mule's appetite by pounding a big cork up its ass."

The class exploded.

What was the bottom line on the CWA? It was a watered-down statute applicable to only a small number of pollutants. Will EPA get into the game? Will additional pollutants be regulated? Will the CWA get beyond Best Practicable Technology? The outlook wasn't particularly promising.

*   *   *

We were now knee deep into the recruiting season and I still hadn't heard from Simoneaux, the New Orleans firm where I had clerked the previous summer. When I ran into Sarah Riley, a 3L with whom I had worked, I thought I might get some sort of update. Sarah was an older student who had returned to school after a number of years as a paramedic. I caught up to her in the parking lot next to the law school. She said she had accepted an offer with another firm, where she had spent the second half of the summer. I was happy for her. She would be practicing health care law, some medical malpractice, areas in which she had an interest.

"I called and told Barbara," she said. "She seemed miffed, but I don't care."

I wanted a little more.

"She acted like she couldn't believe I didn't wait to hear from them."

"I haven't heard anything," I volunteered.

"Has anyone?"

"I heard Alicia got dinked."

"Huh?"

"She didn't get a job offer," I said.

"She told me she hadn't heard yet."

"I just know what Richard told me."

I shouldn't have said anything, I knew that immediately, but we all needed to know where we stood. I think I sought out these conversations to rekindle the sense of camaraderie we all had felt over the summer when we worked out of the same room, car-pooled, ate together, drank together, played together. I didn't expect to be invited back to Simoneaux. The only card I had to play was that I had yet to receive a rejection, and I flashed that card so often sometimes it even looked to me like an ace.

                    *   *   *

At home, I was getting rejection letters in the mail on a regular basis:

Dear Mr. Westphal:

It was a pleasure to meet with you at our Tulane Law School interviews on September 25. Although we were impressed by your credentials, we will be unable to make an offer of employment to you at this time. Our interviewing was made very difficult this year by the number of fine candidates we met.

We sincerely appreciate your interest in Knox, Brandt, Mouledoux & White and we wish you the very best in your legal career.

Very truly yours,

Bernard G. Pidcock

BGP/drn/12

                    *   *   *

Dear Mr. Westphal:

Thank you very much for meeting with us at Tulane Law School during our recent interviews. All of us conducting the interviews were impressed by the number of outstanding men and women who chose to interview with our firm.

In the past several weeks, we have interviewed many fine applicants such as yourself, and the selection process has been extremely difficult. We can hire only those few applicants whose qualifications are closely tailored to our hiring needs and regret that we cannot offer you a position at this time. Please understand that this decision in no sense reflects upon your academic and professional qualifications.

We appreciate your interest in Malone, Swope, Christy, Calumet & Franks and extend our best wishes for success in your legal career.

Very truly yours,
MALONE, SWOPE, CHRISTY,
CALUMET & FRANKS

Julia Louise Overby

/ggr

Nevertheless, I did receive a couple of letters that held some promise. One was from Mr. Andrew Payne, a lawyer whose wife worked with my mother. He had passed my letter and resume to his law firm's Columbus office with the recommendation that the new lawyer committee consider my request "very carefully." The other letter was from Arter & Hadden, the firm where Mark H. McCormick, of sports management fame and author of *What I Should Have Learned at Yale Law School*, had started his career. The oldest firm west of the Appalachians, Arter & Hadden had picked McCormick out of law school and deposited him in a cellar in Montreal, Canada, where he lived like a mole for eighteen months trying to find a document that would link two men to an agreement. I read the Arter & Hadden letter with interest:

Dear Mr. Westphal:

As Director of Legal Recruiting Richard Tate has forwarded your recent letter and accompanying resume expressing an interest in a summer clerk position with Arter & Hadden.

We would be pleased to conduct an interview if you find yourself in the Cleveland area sometime this fall. Please be advised, however, that it is not our policy to reimburse travel expenses for interviews not conducted on-campus.

If you are interested, I would ask that you contact me in order to arrange a convenient date and time. Thank you for your interest in Arter & Hadden. I look forward to hearing from you.

Very truly yours,
ARTER & HADDEN

Tara L. Hansen
Director of Recruiting

TLH/bch:790

Right now, rummaging through musty papers in a cold cellar for $65,000 a year didn't sound so bad. Both Mr. Payne's letter and the letter from Arter & Hadden were nice, but hardly hot prospects. Both were sterling law firms, firms where partners could make close to a million dollars a year. I was scarcely in the top quarter of my class and hadn't polished an attitude of superiority. My attitude was self-defeating, sure, but I knew I would be wasting my time. Too many other people were telling me I was wasting my time, and I didn't have to pay hundreds of dollars in plane fare and take a week off from school to hear it. I got the message delivered to my doorstep daily.

October 11
(Friday)

The one thing I knew about finding a summer job was to get the letters out early, the first week of October at the latest. I had stalled about as long as I could, waiting for some word from the Environmental Law Journal before I wrote Gaines and other Ohio firms. Since the announcement of the new Law Review members, anticipation had been mounting for the ELJ decision. I joined in the countdown. The Law Review competition had ended a week before the ELJ competition, which meant, by my calculation, that by the end of the week we could expect some sort of response. But the week passed without a word. I went ahead and sent letters to some of the larger firms in Columbus. My plan was to blanket Columbus, Cleveland, and Cincinnati, making a special appeal to Tulane graduates working in Ohio.

After Evidence on Friday, I checked again for the ELJ list. Nothing. Still, I had a strong suspicion that this would be the day. Two weeks had passed since the Law Review decision was handed down. This put the ELJ a week behind the pace set by the Law Review. The editors of the ELJ had to have more self respect than to let the contest go on any longer. Surely, they wouldn't let it absorb another weekend. The thing had to come to an end. So at five o'clock on Friday afternoon, I went back to the law school for a look. Katie decided to come along. If the news was good, she knew a celebration would follow.

It was nice to be out of the house on a Friday evening. As an under-graduate, I never studied on Friday night. It was my night at the movies, out to dinner, in front of the TV, doing something, anything but what someone else told me to do. Such preferences had to yield once I started law school. During the first year, an evening not studying was an evening someone else was getting ahead. My loss. October evenings in New Orleans were beautiful once the heat of the day subsided.

I turned on the college radio station and drove. I cut off St. Charles, where people jogged and walked dogs, to Freret Street, where people sat on porches to watch life or gathered on the corner to discuss it. I pushed down slightly on the gas and took the curve in the road like a soft gray, like sand, before finally disappearing.

The law school was deserted, the hallways silent. If there was a posting, it would be on the announcement board inside the main entrance. But I thought there might also be a notice on the door of the ELJ office. And as we turned the corner, I saw the piece of paper taped to the door.

"There it is," I said.

Katie moved in front of me and we took a few steps closer. This was it, all right, a short congratulatory statement followed by about eight names. We didn't dare breathe.

We scanned the names ...

"There I am," I said, pointing to the bottom of the list. Mine was the second to the last name. Now Katie saw the name, too. It was real. She gave me a hug.

"I had prepared myself for a letdown," I said, trying to explain why I felt nothing but relief.

She insisted she fully expected to see my name there. "That's why I was so confused," she said. "I kept scanning the first few names on the list, thinking I'd missed it."

We had scarcely moved, but now our whole lives had shifted slightly. For the rest of my life I could say I had been a member of the Tulane Environmental Law Journal. I had the name of Tulane Law School behind me, which was impressive. Now I had journal experience. I'd had plenty of doubts lately, but now I thought perhaps we were meant to come to New Orleans. Beneath my name in the Martindale-Hubbell, it would say, *Member: Tulane Environmental Law Journal.* It might help to impress clients. It would likely help to get a job. I didn't see how Gaines could turn me down now.

We let all of this sink in as we stood there, looking at the list again and again, reading the words of welcome across the top of the page. But I also wanted to see the list in the main hallway. I wanted to see how it looked on the wall behind glass and to imagine how the rest of the school would see it on Monday morning. So off we went. The ceiling became a twisted canopy of giant oaks, the hallway a green lake, and we spent the rest of the evening taking a stroll through the park like picnickers on plum wine.

8

October 14
(Monday)

There was a memo in my folder from Trisha Stock, the editor-in-chief of the ELJ, welcoming the new members and bringing us up to date on the progress of the first issue. Work was proceeding on schedule. Everyone had done a tremendous job on their "sub and cite," the process of verifying the substance of an article and checking the citations for accuracy and completeness. A mandatory meeting would be held that night at the school, at which time Tony King, the senior articles editor, would describe our casenote assignments.

In my elation at being selected to the ELJ, I had completely forgotten that I'd have to write another casenote before the end of the semester. To receive credit for being on the ELJ, one credit a year, new members had to fulfill certain writing obligations, and the first was the production of a casenote deemed suitable for publication by the ELJ. Topics and deadlines would follow within the week.

*   *   *

The interview with Dunn, Bellington was in The Avenue Hotel, like the other interviews had been, but not in one of the hotel rooms. This interview was in one of the larger conference areas. No refrigerator, no dining room table, no sofa. One look at the interviewer explained everything. He was a sweaty man in his mid-thirties, balding on top. His collar was dirty, his tie crumpled. He didn't trust himself in a hotel room for twenty minutes with a pretty law student, a fresh thing with smiles and sweet smells and slender crossed legs. He couldn't take it. He could hardly take the thought of it. He had two kids, a wife, and was about to be made partner, and he just couldn't take it. So he sat on a folding chair in a room without air conditioning or iced drinks, paying his penance.

I gave him a new resume that listed me as a member of the ELJ. He ripped the other in half and crossed the room to the trash can. "So there won't be any confusion," he said.

He seemed interested in what I had to say, especially about my work at Simoneaux, nodding as he doodled on my resume, circles and shapes, lines upon lines. At first, I couldn't believe what he was doing. That was my resume. That was me lying there, suffering beneath the thick strokes of his pen. I realized I was being silly. At least, I thought, the resume might stand out in some way, perhaps his masterpiece of doodling, something he'd want to frame and put on the wall. At least I might have that much going for me. And he did seem interested in what I had to say.

"Well, it sounds like you had a good experience at Simoneaux," he said. "They're a good bunch. Very good lawyers. I've worked with some of them. It's too bad they had that incident two years ago."

"They've made up for it this year," I said, referring to the anti-trust suit they had just settled.

"There but for the grace of God," he said, looking sweaty. "That little mistake is going to ruin some very good careers." He was talking about the missed filing deadline by Baracci, the law firm on the other side, a mistake which put millions of dollars into the pockets of Simoneaux lawyers. "It could've happened to any lawyer in town."

He was right. The lawyer who had overseen the case for Baracci, Terrence Sisto, had for many years taught Civil Procedure at Louisiana State University. If he could miss a filing deadline, anyone could. Simoneaux had pushed hard. The lawyers counted down the days left for filing in disbelief. Now, several of the lawyers at Simoneaux would become millionaires over again. And the law firm of Baracci, Borne & Sisto, offices in New Orleans, Dallas, and Baton Rouge, would struggle to survive.

"I've heard people say they aren't going to cry for Baracci," I said.

"Sure, they play hardball. That's what it's all about. I don't think they deserve all that's happened to them. It's just too bad…. Is the case over?"

"My understanding is that it's been settled. I think Simoneaux settled for forty-five million. Now all that's left is the malpractice case."

He seemed to shudder.

Overall, the interview had gone smoothly. He had taken my ERISA casenote and promised to read it. He said he had just taken an ERISA case and was trying to learn all he could in a short time. In the hallway on the way out, I passed Francis Penwell, who had the next interview, looking dapper in a green suit, stroking his goatee gently with his fingertips. We nodded. Francis was on the ELJ as well.

*   *   *

"Where is everybody?" Landrow wanted to know. "Is there something going on I don't know about?"

Nobody could come up with any explanation as to why so many people were missing from Evidence, so Landrow told us to put a star in the upper right-hand corner of our notes. These notes, he said, would have special significance on the exam. "So don't lend your notes," he told us. Then he reconsidered: "You can lend your notes but just don't tell anyone the significance of the star."

Landrow really liked people to come to class.

On this significant day, then, we continued our discussion of the "relevance rules," rules which generally bar the admissibility of evidence, often for public policy reasons. Subsequent remedial measures, for example, aren't admitted to show that something is dangerous because the law doesn't want to discourage repairs. The fact that one party has insurance is excluded because it might create bias on the part of the jury to find liability. Settlement offers are excluded because the law wants to encourage frank and open settlement discussions.

*   *   *

At home, the letters continued to arrive:

> Dear Mr. Westphal:
>
> Thank you for your recent inquiry regarding the possibility of working with our firm.
>
> Unfortunately, we are not in a position to offer you employment at this time. We will, however, keep your resume on file in the event our needs should change at some time in the future.
>
> Please accept our best wishes for what promises to be a very successful career in the legal field.
>
> Very truly yours,
WYSS, COOKE, BICHIMERE &
COOKE
>
> Roger A. Sherwin
>
> RAS/cbh

My story was being written by others, one letter at a time. Other students had their own stories to tell. On one of the lockers at school, a

woman posted a letter that soberly informed her the person at the firm
to whom she had written would be unable to help her secure a legal
position at this or any other law firm because he had been dead for two
years. *In Re:*, the law school newspaper, ran a story by a woman who
answered an ad posted at Career Services for a summer job paying six
dollars an hour. Before she would even be considered for the job, she
was shocked to learn, she would have to write a ten-page paper. This
meant, she decided, that the hiring attorney would have potentially
dozens of projects researched without having to pay a penny.

The story read like satire, but the lawyer's name was listed in the
phone book.

I checked.

* * *

That Simoneaux thought it could dust me off without so much as a
polite letter began to grate my nerves. I hadn't been the worst clerk they
had ever seen. Sure, I had been a slow starter. My first project, which
should have been knocked off in a couple of days, took two weeks. I was
supposed to pick up some trash on the edge of a pond and instead I
dragged the bottom—and hadn't done that very well, either. On the
other hand, I finished strong, completing several lengthy projects in the
closing weeks. Just after the start of the semester, I called Todd Hughes,
an associate I had worked with on one of the later assignments, to see
how my work had been received. "We liked your project," he told me,
meaning he and the partner in charge of the case. "It was one of the
finer written pieces we've seen from a clerk. I made that known. I can't
speak for everyone, though. I can't tell you how your chances are."

He was right. Surely there were others who could make a strong case
against me. Evidently they had. Still, I accepted the praise greedily.
There had been other successes, other kind words. Several projects had
been shown directly to clients. I hadn't been the worst clerk in the

world. I kept my pants on. I showed up on Fridays. Who knew what my chances were? I hadn't expected to get the job in the first place and look what happened.

As one of my mentors, Robin would have had to stand up for me at recruiting committee meetings, and I wondered if I could tell from the sound of her voice whether I had been damned with faint praise. At this point, I didn't care if I wasn't going to be asked back. I didn't expect to be asked back. I just wanted to hear something. In my desk with a stack of other phone numbers was Robin's business card. She had given me the card on my last day at Simoneaux, almost as an afterthought. I dialed her direct number and she answered on the second ring.

"I just called to hear your voice," I told her.

"Yeah." She was a little suspicious.

"Well," I said. "I'll get right to it. Have all the hiring decisions been made on the clerks for next summer? I haven't heard anything."

"I think all of the decisions have been made." She was being straightforward, at least. That was how to give bad news. I was sorry now to have given her the chance, but she had already launched into the standard rap. "Like all the other firms, we've cut back on our summer clerk program ..." I shouldn't have called. I was a dog at a picnic and there were steaks on the grill. She had sauce on her chin. "I was under the impression you wanted to return to Ohio," she said. "Are you interviewing with Ohio firms?"

"Yes." I couldn't deny the direct question, but I had been careful never to say anything to her or to anyone else about wanting to return to Ohio. Such a statement would have been suicidal.

"I think the last of the letters were sent out several weeks ago," she went on. "You never received anything?"

"No," I said, weakly. "I haven't received a thing."

"I'll look into it."

I remembered then why I had called. I wanted to let her know I was mentioning names of people I had worked with at Simoneaux to interviewers who asked. If someone was jabbing me in the back, I wanted it to stop. If I didn't get a job, I held Simoneaux responsible. My conversation with Todd Hughes had started me thinking. I wanted to know if I was making a mistake mentioning certain people. Robin didn't seem to understand. I tried to make my point a little more clearly.

"I spoke with Todd Hughes," I told her. "He said he had nothing but nice things to say about my work, but he couldn't speak for everyone at the firm. I need to know if there's anyone whose name at the firm I shouldn't mention when I interview."

"I'm sure you'd get a good reference from the people here," she said.

"Okay." I could hear her thinking. It didn't hurt to let her know I had my suspicions.

"Is there anything else I can do for you?" she asked.

"No, that's it ... oh, hey, I wrote onto the Environmental Law Journal." It felt good to tell her this.

"That's great," she said.

"Yeah. A lot of people were trying to write on. I heard something like a hundred people."

"That's great."

*   *   *

I was standing in the hallway before the ELJ meeting when Kevin St. Germain approached, dressed in a suit for his part in a mock trial for the moot court competition later that evening. He was helping Rosey, one of the participants, by playing the part of the witness. He could have gotten away with a sports jacket, I figured, a shirt and tie, a sweater even, but here he was, walking around the school in his best suit.

At the ELJ meeting, Tom King stood up and talked about the casenotes we'd have to write. He stressed that they had to be of publishable quality. We knew what to do, he said. We'd all been through it before. The big announcement at the meeting, though, was that eight people would be selected as associate editors and their names would appear on the masthead as such. The associate editors would be responsible for subscriptions, reconciliations, and substantive editing of articles, comments, and casenotes. Listening to the job description, I was almost certain that with my background I could get one of the eight positions, so certain in fact that I mentioned it later that evening to my parents. Then I put aside my homework and spent several hours phrasing my one-page statement of interest, polishing it to perfection.

October 15
(Tuesday)

At two minutes after the hour, the door opened and Jose strode into the room, the lapels of his suit flapping lightly at his sides. Worth was in the process of creating a time line on the chalk board and didn't look up.

By now, Worth had called on almost everyone in Remedies at least twice. I had been called on only once, so there was a chance I'd be called on again. Worth seemed conscious of who had spoken. I sat low in my seat. Worth was willing to call on me as little as possible. Still, when it was clearly my turn, he'd have to say my name. My immediate comfort was that Jose had yet to be called on at all. Worth couldn't in good faith call on me with Jose sitting in the same line of sight. I didn't care how low Jose was able to scrunch. It wouldn't be right. I was slouching, too, and people who slouch know the patterns. They record the slow daily discussions. I knew it wasn't my turn just yet, but Worth looked at his seating chart and then at me.

"Mr. Westphal?"

I sat up.

"Yes," he said. "Mr. Westphal. What do you think about ..."

I knew enough to say that a temporary restraining order is granted when the irreparable harm is so imminent that a permanent injunction would be insufficient. I also knew that the standard for TROs is very demanding. But when Worth pressed me on the standard, I had to yield. The spotlight turned. There is no single meaning for "irreparable injury." Irreparable injury is just a catch phrase for various policies. The plaintiff can almost always find something inadequate with the alternative legal remedy ...

I guess I should have said that.

But nobody really cared anymore who said what.

*   *   *

Pollution Control took on new meaning now that I was on the Environmental Law Journal. Although I had considered the idea of being an environmental lawyer, considered pursuing a certificate in environmental law studies, now that I was a member of the ELJ, my goals, my life history, began to rewrite themselves: *I came to Tulane in part for the opportunity to study environmental law with some very highly regarded professors. With both marvelous natural resources and pressing pollution problems, Louisiana is a state where environmental issues often come to the forefront.... I am pursuing what Tulane calls a "certificate in environmental law studies," which requires 15 credit hours of selected environmental law courses, and keeping my research and writing skills sharp by working as an associate editor on the Tulane Environmental Law Journal ...*

Over the next several nights, I sent letters to every environmental lawyer in Columbus, Cleveland, and Cincinnati. My uncle suggested I write to Harry Canton, an environmental lawyer he knew at Fielding & Watt, a Cleveland law firm, and to use the name of Fay Rubenstein by way of introduction. Ms. Rubenstein had worked at Fielding for several years before joining his company. I spent some extra time with that letter. Having someone's name at the top meant that it would be given that much more attention. And I began to dream about living in Cleveland.

In Pollution class, we plunged into a study of water toxics, the most important part of the CWA. The Act contained at least six approaches to water toxics: a health-based effluent standard, effluent limits based on BAT, pretreatment standards, more BAT, biomonitoring, and more water quality standards.

The health-based standard required an "ample margin of safety." But how does the EPA arrive at that number? What is risk assessment? For the chemical endrin, the EPA established the standard on the basis of a 96-hour lab study. It determined that the short-term lethal dose of endrin was .5 parts per billion (ppb). Then, using a dilution factor of 100, the EPA estimated the long-term tolerable concentration.

"Is this scientific?" Muder asked us. "To some extent, it's mere guesswork, soft science. Does it look at synergistic effects? No. Does it look at reproductive effects? Not that I can tell."

So with a long-term standard of .005 ppb, what amount of endrin can be dumped into water so that the most sensitive critter could safely take it into its body? Measuring toxics at the end of the pipe wouldn't be reasonable, so the calculation must allow for a "mixing zone," the area at the end of the pipe where the chemical mixes with water before its concentration is measured. In the case of endrin, the EPA accounted for a mixing zone by multiplying the long-range standard, .005, by a dilution factor of 300 to arrive at an emission standard of 1.5 ppb.

"How did they get the dilution factor of 300?" Muder asked. "Guesswork," she answered. "And this is guesswork that can cost industry millions. In the *Hercules* case, the court deferred to the EPA on every scientific assumption."

The striking thing about mixing zones, one of the greatest factors determining what the impact of the discharge on water will be, is that they vary from state to state. There is no standard for what is appropriate. Louisiana, for example, has a tiny mixing zone for toxins. To calculate what comes out of the pipe, then, one must resort to a formula that accounts for a variety of variables. Louisiana's formula looks like this:

$C2 = [(Q1 + Q2) * C—Q1 * C1]$.

Variables include the size of the mixing zone, the cleanliness of the water upstream, and the total flow of the water.

That the total flow of water entered the equation was painful to Muder. "You could drop a tank into the Mississippi and it would get lost," she said.

"What happens if you can't pollute any more?" someone asked.

"You mean, what happens if the water is so polluted that any more pollution would completely shut down industry?"

"Yeah."

"One word," Muder said, pausing for emphasis: "Bubbles."

Huh? We looked at each other with stupid smiles.

"We'll talk about it later," Muder said, pushing us back. "For now, just think: Bubbles."

*   *   *

In Business Enterprises, Tarenzella called on me, finally, about six weeks into the semester. We were discussing the governing law of the corporation: state statutes, federal securities laws, state securities laws. She launched into a long hypothetical about a close corporation whose majority owners created and then transferred assets to a subsidiary, then issued stock in the subsidiary corporation. The majority owners planned to use some of the stock to raise cash, loan this cash to themselves to buy the remaining shares, and thus dilute the ownership of the minority.

I was still trying to take down the facts when Tarenzella began asking questions: Is the transaction authorized under the statute? What about a decision to close a plant? Can the corporation sell all or substantially all of its assets without shareholder approval? Can a corporation own shares in another corporation? To create a subsidiary, what does the close corporation have to do? How does this affect the minority owner of the close corporation?

"Let's go to a new face," she said.

The camera panned the classroom, close to a hundred nameless faces, focused with a quick and somewhat sickly zoom on one, a face with neither character nor style, a bare lonely plain insignificant face: my face.

"Mr. Westphal?"

"I don't know," I said. I suppose at some point I had planned just such a response in just such a situation, but it was nothing conscious. The words came out as naturally as a giggle. I wasn't even sure what she had asked, but I knew I didn't have the answer and that repeating the question wouldn't help. I didn't know.

Tarenzella was ready to pounce. The words were on her lips, *Come on, now, Mr. Westphal. You can't tell that to a client: "I don't know, man, why don't you get an attorney." This is easy. Even Perry Mason could do it....* But before she could attack, Francis Penwell's hand was in the air.

"Yes, Francis," she said.

He said something about the minority owner's pre-emptive rights.

"Right," she said, elaborating on something I did not yet understand.

*   *   *

That afternoon, I was surprised to pick up the telephone and hear the voice of Kimball Donilan, the recruiting coordinator at Gaines.

"We're still in the process of making decisions," she told me. "I didn't want you to think we'd fallen off the face of the earth."

Over the past couple of weeks, I had begun to wonder. Had I been wrong in thinking I'd be invited back to Gaines in October? Had I made a mistake in mentioning that I looked forward to seeing them again? It was a good sign that she had called. The wheels of progress were turning slowly. The decision, she guessed, would be made in the next week or so.

"I'm glad you called," I said. "I have good news: I'm now on the Environmental Law Journal. I just heard the other day. There was a writing competition."

"Well, you're a good writer."

"I hope you can take that into account when you make your decision," I said.

"I'll certainly pass that along."

That afternoon, I put together a package to send her: a cover letter, a new resume, and a copy of the ELJ. I bought a special envelope to mail it in and sent it off the next day.

October 17
(Thursday)

When I got home from school Thursday, there was a message on my answering machine from Robin. She would try to reach me later. The call was another surprise, and I took it as a good sign, a very good sign. Had she called to make me a job offer at Simoneaux? I couldn't figure out any other reason. She had spoken with Christian Ressner, I imagined. Although Simoneaux had a Recruiting Committee, it was Ressner who really made the hiring decisions. Robin had given him the gist of our conversation: I hadn't received a letter, I was still looking for work, I half suspected they weren't doing all they could to help me out. He thought it over and gave her an answer. Robin listened and nodded. After all, my uncle was a big client. Now she was calling to give me the good news and to smooth any rough spots left from our conversation a few days before. All I had to do was push the right button, just a little pressure at the right place at the right time ...

I couldn't wait. I called her office. Her secretary said she was in a meeting and wouldn't be back until after lunch. I played the message on the answering machine again. Robin spoke fast. She said "bye" at the end in a pleasant way. I could tell she was smiling. She was trying to make up. I listened to the message again.

"This is good," I told Katie. "The only possible reason Robin could have for calling was to make me an offer." I couldn't conceive any other reason for her to call. She would try to reach me later. There was some urgency. There was some sense of reaching out. It was all captured on my answering machine, the message, Robin, all of it. I tried again to reach her before I left for Pollution Control, but she was still out. "No message," I said. "I'll try again at four o'clock."

When I came home, I found a letter from Simoneaux in the mailbox. I set my books on my desk and opened it as I stood in the kitchen:

> Dear Kenneth:
>
> I would like to take this opportunity to thank you for the good work you did for the firm in our clerkship program this summer.
>
> After some deliberation and discussion with our managing partners and personnel committee members regarding the size and aims of next summer's program, we have concluded that we must decrease significantly the size of next summer's program. In that regard we are urged to target those students with a definite expressed intent to practice in New Orleans after graduation from law school. In other years the criteria for our decisions would be significantly broader; however, at this time regrettably we are unable to offer you a position in the coming summer program.
>
> I hope that the experience you gained with us this past summer was a positive step in your professional development. We will be happy to furnish recommendations regarding your work to potential employers

who contact us for references, and we wish you a successful second year at Tulane.

With kindest regards,

Sincerely yours,

Christian T. Ressner
Chairman, Personnel
Committee

He signed the letter "Chris." What a nicely written letter, I thought. Well-phrased. Logic wrapped in sincerity and sorrow. Here it was, finally. I wasn't entirely disappointed. The people at the firm knew I was still looking for a job. They had promised recommendations. And they would presumably toe the line that I hadn't been asked back because I couldn't give a definite expressed intention to remain in New Orleans. They would know what to say when asked. Better yet, I would know what they would say.

"They must have rushed this one out to the mail to get it here this quickly," I told Katie. "They must have had a courier hand-deliver it to the post office."

Katie muttered something that surprised me.

"I wonder what Robin wants," I said.

I called her. Perhaps there was some mistake.

"Have you received the letter?" she asked.

"Yes."

"I wanted to talk to you before you got it," she said. "I wanted to tell you, if I can help in any way, as a reference or in any other way, just let me know."

"That's very nice of you," I said. "Thank you very much."

Well, I never really expected to be invited back. I just wanted to shake the tree and see if I could get any figs to fall. If I couldn't get a job now …

9

October 18
(Friday)

I watched television for a few minutes in the lounge before going up to Remedies and a sparsely filled classroom.

People frequently came to Remedies unprepared. As a result, Worth's podium before the start of class was always covered with excuses of one sort or another. I gave into the temptation on a number of occasions as well, always printing my note, even my own name at the bottom, so Worth would have no writing sample when it came time to grade the exams. By the end of the semester, a professor teaching a small class has some idea who grasps the material and who is in trouble. Knowing who wrote which exam would make grading them that much easier, and anything that made grading exams easier would be something of interest to a law professor, especially someone like Nathan Worth, who seemed more than most to enjoy his escape from the bigtime practice of law.

I also had been careful not to leave too many notes because I suspected I might need Worth as a reference some day. He was my academic advisor, after all, although I had yet to seek him out for advice. I wasn't one to visit professors in their offices or to linger after class with questions, so I hadn't gotten to know any of my professors very well. He was all I had. And after several notes in quick succession, I tried to give this most recent one a sense of self-castigation: "Unprepared. I hope this will be the last time. Kenneth Westphal."

Jose saw my note when he dropped his onto the pile. I watched him thumb through the stack on the podium.

"I saw your note," he said, sitting down behind me. "Good one."

"Yeah."

"'I hope this will be the last time,'" Jose said, having too much fun and speaking far too loudly. "That's good.... I'll have to use it myself some time."

Funny guy.

*   *   *

That night, Katie and I went to one of the "Bar Review" parties sponsored by Tulane, regular events that had nothing to do with studying for the bar exam. This week's party was at FM, a nightclub on Tchoupitoulis. The free kegs were empty by the time we arrived, so I ordered beers at the bar and we went out on the patio to sit in the open air.

After awhile, Rosey wandered through. We were talking to her about New York, where she was from, when Jose stopped by.

"Rosey, this is Jose," I said.

Jose held out his arms. He took hold of Rosey and kissed her.

"Nice to meet you," he said.

"Nice to meet you," she said.

"So nice to meet you."

More kisses.

I felt foolish. They obviously knew each other quite well. I left them kissing and went off to find a bathroom. The place was packed. Law students everywhere. When I came back I found a pitcher of beer on our table and a full glass in front of me.

"Jose bought us a pitcher," Katie said.

"What do you think about that?"

"I think you owe him some notes."

"Yeah. But how many? How many notes is a pitcher of beer worth?"

October 20
(Saturday)

Madeline Matthews, one of the senior members of the ELJ, left a message on my answering machine that I had been named an associate editor. I called her back.

"Where have you been?" she asked. That was nice. She liked my statement of interest.

I was making the change to my resume later that night when Betty Goodwin, the senior managing editor, called and asked me to edit a casenote.

"It's by a student," she said. "It needs a lot of work. I mean, it's not even right."

"Okay."

"I've just got to ask you one favor," she said. "Don't tell anyone you're doing this. It could ruffle some feathers. I'd do it myself but I'm swamped."

"I'd be happy to."

The casenote was in my folder on Sunday.

That afternoon, she called me again, very apologetic. "Please forget I said those things about the casenote," she told me. "You're probably Brad Stoll's best friend."

"I don't know Brad Stoll."

"Well, just forget I said anything. I was too hard on the paper. Just read it through to make sure it's right."

October 21
(Monday)

The Compadre Club of New Orleans had announced that it was soliciting resumes. I added mine to the pile in a box on a shelf in Career

Services. The Compadre Club. The legal community meets the Boy Scouts. Law jobs don't come much more environmentally sound. I had visions of high grass and wide-open spaces. Lawyers on horseback.

"I saw your letter to the Compadre Club," Tommy told me when I sat down in Pollution Control.

I didn't understand immediately.

"Didn't you apply to the Compadre Club?" he asked. "I saw your letter at Career Services."

"I put it at the bottom of the box," I said. Sometimes I did that.

"No," he said. "It was on top."

I didn't like the idea that he had seen my letter. It was too easy for him to glance at my resume underneath. I tried to keep my grade-point average to myself. Still, people who thought about such things would have an idea where I stood. I wasn't on Law Review or Moot Court, which meant that I wasn't in the top ten or fifteen percent of the class. But by the number of interviews I was getting, I couldn't be too far off. Was I in the top quarter? top third? At least the details were nobody's business but my own.

Or so I hoped.

October 23
(Wednesday)

After the rejection letter arrived from April Newton's old law firm, I decided to mail my casenote to April Newton herself. I called Kerber and asked the receptionist for the name of her new firm. She gave me an answer without missing a beat: Peabody, Newton, & Young. Kerber was showing no hard feelings. Consummate professionals. No big deal.

I re-read the opening lines of my casenote: "On October 26, 1986, New Orleans police found the body of James LaFleur in his car. He had been shot twice." She would at least start it. I had a better chance with a small firm, anyway. If they had just opened their doors, they probably hadn't given much thought to a law clerk. They might need some help over the summer. And April Newton would be in a position to hire me on the spot. A week later I received an invitation to meet with her at the firm.

The lobby of the offices of Peabody, Newton & Young was small, still in the process of being put together. The rug curled up in the corner. Some painting remained to be done. Books were needed to fill empty shelves. But the essentials seemed to be in place. The receptionist sat behind her desk. Coffee was brewing. They were open for business.

I was admiring an oil painting on the wall when April Newton walked in, an attractive woman of about fifty. She looked a little fragile, but I imagined she was often described as elegant.

"Let's go back to my office," she said.

I was used to large firms where we arrived at the interviewer's office only after passing through a maze. Her office was a few steps away, across the hall from the lobby. On the wall behind her desk was a picture of herself with U.S. Representative Pat Schroeder. They both looked amused and a little put out by the photographer.

I said something about how exciting it must be to start a new practice. She nodded. Why would three partners leave high-paying jobs at one of the best firms in the city to start their own firm? More money? Control? Prestige? Power? Spite? Power? Money? They had likely brought most of their clients along. The idea of the same service and lower fees was quite persuasive.

It was not infrequent for big-name partners to go where the grass was greener. Kerber just seemed to be suffering more than its share of defections in recent years. Only the year before, I came to learn, Michael Ruehl had left to join Glennon, Moid, taking with him the *Times-Picayune*, New Orleans' morning newspaper, a huge client. The law firm scrambles, reorganizes, but survives. The ones really hurt are the associates the big partner has driven like slaves for three or four years who aren't invited to the party.

"My old resume is a little out of date," I said, handing her a new one. "Since then, I've joined the Environmental Law Journal. I'm now associate editor."

"That's wonderful," she said, looking at my resume and taking a seat. "I enjoyed your casenote very much. There's been a development in *LaFleur* since we last spoke. I don't know if you've heard. The Supreme Court has granted *certiorari* and Connecticut General has picked up Washington counsel. They probably figure Washington counsel has better connections, I suppose."

I didn't grasp immediately what she was telling me. The Supreme Court was good. *Certiorari* was good. That meant the case would continue. But was she out of the picture now that Washington counsel had been hired? Was I? Evidently so. Yet she hadn't canceled the interview. I was sitting in her office.

"Are you interested in practicing environmental law?" she asked.

"Yes, I am." What could I say? I had written an ERISA casenote to get on the ELJ, and now I was feeling the squeeze of my own success. But few people who claim to be environmental lawyers can practice environmental law exclusively. It's best to have a fallback. That was my rallying cry.

"The place to go with environmental law is Freeport," she said. "They're on the cutting edge of environmental law. I don't mean to imply there's not necessarily a summer job here. As I mentioned in my letter, we just don't know yet what our hiring needs will be. But if you're interested in environmental law, you might consider applying to Freeport."

I nodded. Although her words had been carefully chosen, such talk was depressing. I knew that not every interview would lead to a job offer, but at least I wanted a week or two to dream. Good interviews give you a chance. Besides, I wanted the firm to covet me. I wanted the thought of my going anywhere else to keep them up at night. I certainly didn't want the possibility of my working elsewhere openly discussed, evaluated, encouraged. Interviewers may think they're helping a student by mentioning other places to apply for work, but the practice seems nothing short of sadistic. Of course, mentioning an area of interest outside the firm's practice area is just asking for abuse. Perhaps we should have both shown up for the interview in leather and chains. No sense playing hard to get.

As she spoke, I listened with the sickening sense that recruiting season was rapidly nearing an end. I would have been interested if she had told me to mention her name or to tell so-and-so, an old friend. Then I might not have minded the good-natured advice. In fact, I would have been delighted. But as it was, I couldn't shake the feeling that I was being handed to someone else and in the process in grave danger of being dropped.

She gave me a tour of the offices and introduced me to the other two attorneys as the person who had written the casenote on *LaFleur*. One of the lawyers said, "Nice job." For a moment, all of us were gathered in one office, the entire firm and me. Coffee. The morning sun rising. The start of something big. April Newton tried to describe the editorial cartoon in the morning's *Times-Picayune*, but she got the point mixed up and the moment passed.

She took me around the corner to their file room. Wall to wall files. These attorneys had evidently brought along every file, every blessed note they had made, over the past twenty years of practice.

*   *   *

That afternoon Tarenzella ended class saying we should read the material on limited partnerships, which produced a general mumbling among the class. I hadn't looked ahead at the material, so I looked to Tommy to see what all the fuss was about.

"It's one hundred pages," Tommy told me.

Tarenzella turned the pages of her book as if she were reconsidering. "Read it all," she decided, shutting the book. "We've got to get going."

There was a collective groan as people packed their books.

"Just read it," she said. "It's not that important anymore, anyway. Does anyone know why limited partnerships aren't as important as they once were?"

Someone said, "Because the tax law has changed."

"Right."

As it turned out, to do the assignment we also had to read the Limited Partnership Act and the Revised Limited Partnership Act. Some states had adopted one and not the other. I wondered if I would have time to read any of it.

*   *   *

For the ELJ, I was assigned to write a casenote on *Transportation Leasing Co. v. California*, a CERCLA case. A federal court required a number of cities to help pay for the cleanup of a landfill they had used. Between 1974 and 1984, 29 cities deposited their municipal solid waste in the Monterey, California, landfill. When the site was included on CERCLA's National Priorities List, cleanup costs were estimated at between $500 million and $800 million. The cities sought a ruling that the waste generated by local residences and businesses was excluded from CERCLA's definition of "hazardous substances." The cities lost. Plenty of stuff in the average household wastebasket qualifies as hazardous or at least becomes hazardous over time.

Having been through one casenote before, at least I knew where to start. And as I began my research, my opinion in favor of the decision began to take shape rather quickly. Environmentalists liked the decision. Industry liked the decision. And the holding clearly advanced the purposes of CERCLA itself, to spread costs and clean up landfills. The discussion of the background of the case would focus on the sloppy definition of "hazardous substances" in the Act, a result of the haste with which Congress had passed CERCLA, and the conclusion would note that local governments had already organized in an attempt to revise CERCLA so municipal solid waste might be treated more "equitably."

Still, the paper would manage to gobble up substantial chunks of two weekends.

*   *   *

One constant throughout the semester was the mail: *At this time our needs for a summer law clerk are uncertain.... I am sorry to say that we will not be able to offer you a job.... We do not have a need for someone with your interest and background at this time....* That sort of thing. Finally, I received a pleasant surprise from a New Orleans firm:

> Dear Mr. Westphal:
>
> Thank you for your resume from the Office of Career Services at Tulane Law School expressing an interest in a summer clerkship position with our firm. We would be pleased to discuss the matter with you further, and suggest that you call me to arrange a mutually convenient time for an interview. We appreciate your interest in our firm and look forward to meeting with you.
>
> Very truly yours,
>
> Muriel Cahn
>
> MC:dgl
> 06540020\931.JAA\Interview.ltr

The firm was Hanssen, Hess, Knarr & Stern. The name meant nothing to me. I counted the number of attorneys on the masthead: twenty-five partners and nine associates. Not bad. Something to do.

I called and set up an interview. We would meet at their offices. It certainly looked promising.

Now I just had to learn a thing or two about the firm.

October 25
(Friday)

"Did you get an interview?" Tommy asked me.

After Evidence, as several of us gathered to talk, I learned that Tommy had been overlooked by the Compadre Club. Not even an interview. Others had gotten interviews—Francis Penwell, for one. Tommy seemed to be taking an informal survey.

I couldn't answer. I hadn't checked my folder before class, so after we broke up I went downstairs to take a look. In my folder I found a notice from Career Services saying that I had been granted an interview with the Compadre Legal Defense Fund in New Orleans. Some helpful information about the Compadre Club was attached. The Legal Defense Fund, I read, is a national, nonprofit law firm, representing clients much as would any other law firm, except that the Legal Defense Fund doesn't charge its clients attorney fees. The credentials of the people in the Louisiana office were impressive. The managing attorney had been Order of the Coif, editor of the Louisiana State Law Review, and for eight years a litigation attorney with a giant Baton Rouge firm. Her staff included a former editor of the Mississippi Law Journal and a graduate of Virginia who had worked for firms in Washington, D.C., Seattle, and New Orleans. A good bunch. I was eager to join.

I ran into Tommy later in the copy room of the library.

"Did you get an interview?" he wanted to know.

"Yeah."

He thought about it a moment. He looked disgusted. He was on the Law Review. He had the science degree, the house, the dog. I had a better grade-point, but my resume, overall, was not that much better than his. He couldn't understand it.

"I met Terry Bantock," he said.

"He's a nice guy." Bantock was one of the 3Ls I had worked with at Simoneaux, also a member of the Law Review.

"He told me you said to give me a hard time," Tommy said, not really looking at me.

"Yeah," I said, "like push you in the pool."

Tommy smiled despite himself. "Lock me out of the sauna," he joked. "Yeah."

*   *   *

Dear Mr. Westphal:

Thanks for your letter of October 11th expressing interest in the firm. Our environmental practice is comprised of toxic tort litigation, insurance coverage issues, and real estate transactions. We do not have a significant regulatory practice before the Ohio EPA.

I have referred your excellent resume to Ted Chatwin, who is our hiring and recruiting partner. If you have a continuing interest in the firm and do not hear from us, you should give him a call.

Very truly yours,

Phillip T. Rendell

PTR:wkb
cc: Ted Chatwin

*   *   *

Betty liked the changes I had made to the student casenote, and Trisha, the editor, called to ask if I'd go over an article for her as well, which turned out to be about "environmental racism." The author made the claim that the Baton Rouge City Council was racist in locating a chemical plant in a section populated by a high percentage of minority citizens. I tried to improve the article where I could.

October 26
(Saturday)

The return address on the envelope was that of Folger, Hawkins, Burke and Howland, one of the firms I had interviewed with before the start of the semester. How strange, I thought. Perhaps they reconsidered. Perhaps none of their draft choices had signed.

> Dear Mr. Westphal:
> Thank you for your resume and letter dated October 11, addressed to Phyllis Whitney formerly of our Columbus office.
> However, as I informed you in my letter of September 17, we had concluded after your meeting with Andy Hewitt and Ollie Volgorad that we were not in a position to invite you back for additional interviews. Unfortunately, our decision has not changed in this regard.
> Best of luck in your second year at Tulane.
> Very truly yours,
>
> Phillip C. Korovin
> Hiring Committee Chairman
>
> PCK:bjs/102291/00557

First I was embarrassed. Then I laughed. Then I wrote "OOPS!" across the top and put the letter on the refrigerator for Katie to see. Somewhere along the line I became a little annoyed. Something about the tone of the letter. It was probably just weariness coming through, but it seemed too brusque given what should have been obvious: I didn't know Phyllis Whitney had been a member of Folger. I had gotten her name from a listing of environmental lawyers, looked her up in the Martindale-Hubbell, which, for whatever reason, hadn't said anything about Folger. I was surprised he had replied at all. The fact that he had taken the time to dictate a letter was a little worrisome. Who did he think I was? What did he think was going on? Was this a Marx Brothers sketch where, after I'm thrown out of the party, I don a different jacket and attempt to walk through the front door again with the invited guests, already eyeing the glorious banquet, a shocked expression on my face when I'm grabbed from behind and escorted out the door by the seat of my pants?

Well was it?

October 28
(Monday)

I had a busy day planned. First, I would meet with the Compadre Club at The Avenue Hotel at nine o'clock. The interview would last twenty minutes. Then I would drive downtown to the offices of Hanssen, Hess for an eleven o'clock interview. I would have just enough time to change before going to B.E. at one o'clock.

I'd had high hopes for the Compadre Club interview, but it just came and went. Nothing. It turned out to be completely ordinary, and sickeningly so. These ordinary interviews were beginning to bother me. I was going into one interview after another with the sole intention of not making mistakes. The questions I was being asked, simple questions about my background, made me feel like a contestant in a beauty pageant. I could smile and laugh but it could only go so far.

I was interviewed by Shannon Jackson, the managing partner. Her credentials had certainly impressed me. Only recently had I come to understand how significant it was to be selected to the Order of the Coif. It meant that the student not only maintained excellent grades, but also impressed the faculty on a daily basis. This was an achievement. Such a student has both the ability to put the course together as a whole, as well as the ability to understand and articulate the subtle arguments that come up day-to-day but simply cannot be tested in a three-hour exam. Such a person could see both the forest and the trees. Such a person would be an excellent lawyer, and, I thought, a good person to work with and learn from. Besides, it was the Compadre Club. It would drive my uncle crazy.

Shannon Jackson could have spent her career as a partner for any law firm in the city but she had chosen to work in the public interest. I tried to figure out what made her tick. Was she really interested in the environment? Was she interested in a nine to five job? Was she fed up with the rat race, the clients, the billing, the politics? Was she worried about her soul? I gambled on the fact that she was finally doing what she had always wanted to do—and doing it with a vengeance. She referred to Muder with obvious affection. I pegged her as the dedicated environmentalist, and I was ready for the march. When she asked me about my work at Simoneaux, Troy & Walters over the previous summer, I told her, "I'm a competitor.... I like to win." I had waited for a chance to say it, and I said it. Now we just looked at each other, both startled by the sudden noise.

Can he be serious?

Didn't she want to beat hell out of corporate America?

How is being competitive supposed to set him apart from half the students in law school? Would he stop at nothing? Was he putting down the more relaxed members of the Environmental Law Journal? What exactly is he trying to say?

What exactly am I trying to say?

And the interview went on from there—suspicion on her part, uncertainty on mine.

But I wanted to work for the Compadre Club. And I was competitive. I made one more attempt. "You do press releases, I assume," I said. This was my second plan of attack, to stress my journalism background.

"We have one going out today," she said.

"I did a lot of that sort of work as an undergraduate. I'd be interested in helping wherever I could to put together press releases. I think that would be a good way to use my legal training. In fact, that's the only way I'm convinced real change will come about, in changing public attitudes, making people aware how different laws affect them. I enjoy putting the law in those terms."

Her reply, although several questions later, came when she told me that the Compadre Club had only two positions available.

I shook my head in bewilderment. "That's amazing," I said. "I didn't know these jobs were so hard to come by. I guess I'm lucky to even have an interview."

"It means something," she said. "I looked at a number of very impressive resumes."

She means Tommy; he has the science background.

There was that guy who taught high school biology ...

What she was saying was true, getting the interview was something. But getting the interview just wasn't enough.

*   *   *

"To what," the interviewer said, "do you attribute your success?" It was an awkwardly worded sentence, forced out after a pause. I was in a conference room of the offices of Hanssen, Hess, on the 14th floor of an office tower on the edge of the Central Business District, a short walk from the Superdome. The interviewer was a young man, about my age, with thick black hair. He was stocky, but his gray suit hung as if he had just lost twenty pounds. He was impressed that last spring I'd had a 3.47 G.P.A., ranking me for the semester near the top ten percent of my class.

"I never saw three-point," he admitted.

I was surprised. Here was a guy, about my age, a couple of years out of law school, making good money working in a high rise building, and he had never seen three-point. The city had to be filled with Tulane graduates who never saw three-point. I was probably being interviewed by them all the time.

"While others studied," he said, "I went out."

I mumbled agreement, still trying to figure out how he had gotten the job never having seen three-point. I knew his father was a partner at Malone, Swope. He told me as much at the start of the interview.

"Did you interview with Malone, Swope?" he had asked.

"Yes."

"I thought so," he said. "My father is with Malone. He said he thought you interviewed with them."

"Did your father do the interview?"

He shook his head. That was something in my favor, I figured. I tried to remember the interview with Malone, Swope. I thought it might have been the one that ended with me trying to explain the relevance of ERISA to environmental law. Then again, it might have been the one to which I had arrived late. At any rate, Malone, Swope was a very good firm. I wondered how my name had come up. Perhaps over dinner the night before. The kid still went to his parents' house for dinner. Perhaps he still lived with them. Or perhaps he had spoken with his father over the phone that morning. Hanssen was letting him do an interview. That was news worth passing along.

—Say, I'm interviewing a summer clerk candidate tomorrow.

—Yeah, do you have a name?

—A guy named, let me see, I have the name right here: Kenneth Westphal.

—Oh, I know that name, he interviewed with us ...

I finally decided he was just making smalltalk. The fact that I had gotten an interview with Malone said something about my credentials.

Perhaps there was no sense to the statement, an awkward attempt to put me at ease. But when he said he had never seen three-point, it occurred to me that having a father as a partner at one of the city's largest law firms might not hurt a legal career. The family would have connections. There might be uncles, neighbors, law school buddies. There might be business tossed his way when conflicts of interest arose.

To what did I attribute my success? Hard work. Common sense. Luck. Good writing skills. The ability to write fast, to write legibly. I could have said a number of things, given him a number of modest explanations. How did a guy who scored 159 on the LSAT, better than three-quarters of those who took the test but scarcely average among those enrolling at Tulane, get spring semester grades better than almost 90 percent of his class?

"I got the hang of taking law school tests, I guess," I said.

He gave an understanding smile.

"You realize after taking a few of these things," I went on, "that there are really few surprises. You know what they're going to ask. If you study the Dormant Commerce Clause for two weeks, you know there's going to be a Dormant Commerce Clause question on the exam. You know it. Once I figured that out it became … sort of … easy."

I saw immediately I had gone too far. I had uttered a bad word. He was unable to stop me. No one could have stopped me. I looked up to see how bad the situation was. He was blushing. I don't know what I said next. It didn't matter. He gave me a tour of their offices. It was the quietest law firm I had ever been in. We went from door to door. Almost everyone was out to lunch. When an attorney was in, we would shake hands. I would say something about how nice it was to meet them. They would say it was nice to meet me. At one point, noting how pleasant it was to meet at a law firm rather than in a hotel, I joked that during my last interview I took a wrong turn and was grilled for twenty minutes by *tourists*. The woman behind the desk just looked at me …

Back out in the lobby, I couldn't think of a single reason why this guy would ever want to work with me. He wouldn't be tortured for long. I would be gone soon enough. He would make sure that I wouldn't be back. I would walk out of the office and onto the street and he would go back to his well-paying job and his view of the Superdome. He would complete a summary of our interview, dictate a rejection letter, and fiddle with some files that had been on his desk a little too long. That night, over dinner, he'd tell his father that he enjoyed filling in for Charles Roudeax. He just might enjoy being a member of the firm's Hiring Committee, he would say. It was fun, a nice break, work he thought he would enjoy. He would be good at it, too. Real good. It all just sort of came easy to him.

I was at Hanssen much longer than I had planned. By the time the interview was over, I had twenty minutes to get home, change clothes, drive to school, park, and get to class. I thought I could make it, but with fifteen minutes to go, I began to consider cutting corners, even wearing my suit to class. Others wore their suits to school during interview season. Some had jobs after class. I could take off my jacket and tie easy enough.

By the time I was at my apartment and running up the stairs, I had almost decided to wear the suit. Twelve minutes. High gear. I could change and make it. I threw on pants, shoes, shirt. I had to use the bathroom. I shouldn't have had that soft drink at the interview. Ten minutes. My heart sank. I had never made it to class in ten minutes, and Tarenzella went crazy when the classroom door opened and interrupted her train of thought. I had already used up my quota of late days. As far as I was concerned, she had no right to stop class the first time a person was late, but perhaps the second, the third ... that was a different story. She had the idea, and she may have been right, that such behavior was just plain rude.

Nine minutes. I was in the car. There was always the chance. I found a parking place with two minutes to go. From where I parked, I still had a five-minute walk. But it wasn't one o'clock yet. I started to run. First a few awkward churns, then a trot. Running across campus is one of the most degrading things a student can do. A friend of mine growing up once claimed that he never ran to class. He just wouldn't do it. It didn't matter how late he was. His motivating words came back to me as I trotted to class, trying to ignore the occasional gawker. I was almost to the law school. I looked at my watch. One o'clock on the nose. I'd be late. I made an effort to run again. I took the stairs two at a time with enough force to knock someone down. The stairway was empty. The hallway was empty. At the end of the hall, I could see the door to B.E. was shut. I was walking now, breathing hard. Class was in session. What a waste. I glanced through the window in the door as I passed. Tommy and Francis had their attention directed to the front of the room. Things were going on without me. I looked again at my watch. Two minutes past. Sheeze. I stood in the hall wondering if someone else would be late. We could go in together. But no one was coming. No one cared. I didn't care. I began to feel stupid waiting around.

I walked outside with remote, sullen steps. People were learning, and I was falling farther and farther behind. On the way to my car, I passed the site of the new chemistry building, a big hole in the ground surrounded by barbed-wire fence. Men in white hard hats on giant machinery maneuvered sewage pipes wide enough for a car to pass through. We lived and worked in big beautiful buildings, walked on paved streets, and beneath us flowed a river of sewage.

I tried to make myself feel better. At least I could treat myself to lunch. Lunch would be a nice treat. After all, I told myself, the interview hadn't gone that badly.

* * *

Tommy didn't volunteer his notes from B.E., and I didn't ask. It didn't help that he had been put in the hot seat that day. My name had been

called, but of course I wasn't there. Tarenzella just moved down the row
to the next person on the seating chart and the camera caught his face
in freeze frame.

*   *   *

I followed up the Compadre Club interview with a letter reiterating
my dedication to environmental law. I would have been a dedicated
advocate, too, but why was I telling her this? How would this help me
get the job? I decided I had completely misinterpreted her motivations.
She relinquished the high-pressure life of a large law firm, gave up a
large salary, and in return she wanted to feel good about herself. She
didn't need people like me around. She needed a laugh.

"Francis got the Compadre Club job," Jonathan told me later.

"Yeah?"

That was my clue. Now I understood. Francis Penwell had the job
almost from the moment he walked in.

"Why do you want to work for the Compadre Club?" she asked him.

He smiled. "My interviews have been ending lately with people
telling me, 'You know, you should try the Compadre Club …' I started
to think they might be right."

She laughed. She had to laugh. That goatee, that forest green suit, he
did look like he belonged with the Compadre Club. She had to almost
suspect that if she bent down and looked beneath the desk, she would
see that, yes, as she thought, on his feet was a pair of huaraches. Yes, he
belonged with the Compadre Club. He could relax.

He smiled again.

Yes, his smile was charming, his goatee rather attractive. They could
all relax and complain over a glass of wine about forces that were all
but immutable.

10

By the end of October, according to Career Services, nearly 1500 "on campus" interviews had taken place at Tulane. Approximately 311 students had met with more than 118 employers to discuss the possibility of summer employment. That meant, on average, each employer had spoken with an average of about thirteen students. All other things being equal, each student would have attended about four interviews.

But all other things were not equal.

The memo was upbeat. The general idea was that many students had prepared well and were approaching their job searches "realistically"—a major theme of Career Services—and should not be discouraged if their efforts didn't produce instant results. Be realistic. Be patient.... At the bottom was a reference to the school's new counseling program: "Based on feedback from students, these sessions have produced excellent results including redrafting of resumes, carefully creating job search plans, and completely reworking interview methods." I added the memo to the recycling bin with a stack of others. Someone had scrawled across the bottom of one in blue ink, "Any jobs?"

October 30
(Wednesday)

Landrow had scheduled a make-up class the night before Halloween. When I arrived, I found a party already in full swing.

People were slapping pizzas onto paper plates, laughing, sticking cups under a beer tap at the front of the room. All of it a complete, pleasant surprise.

"Okay, get some pizza and beer and take your seats," Landrow announced, slapping his hands. "Let's get started. Feel free to come down and help yourself as we speak.... We might be able to wrap up a little early, but we've got some material to cover first."

No one was moving very fast. I helped myself to dinner and took my seat in the rafters to enjoy it. I had room to spread out. As with most make-up classes, a number of students were absent for one reason or another. They may have forgotten. They may have figured someone else's notes were good enough. They may have had another commitment or reasoned that the professor couldn't in good conscience base an exam question on a class scheduled when they may very well have had other legitimate commitments.

"Where's Ted?" I asked Jonathan.

"He swore the make-up was at seven."

Although Landrow had told us to help ourselves to food and drink during class, no one did. There wasn't time. Landrow took off like a demon. Over the next sixty minutes he covered the topic of general character evidence. He told us about collateral issues. He explained impeachment for bias. He showed how one proves bias under the Federal Rules and under the common law. He must have marched through a dozen questions. There was no letting up.

When it was over, I felt like I'd been through an exam. My hand was so cramped I had trouble making it open and close. Phil Miller, a member of the Law Review, asked me in the beer line if I'd gotten everything down. I shook my hand and laughed. It had been a grueling pace. On many points I had scarcely any idea of what Landrow had been rattling on about, but I got it down, every word. I would just have to make sense of it later.

Jonathan said, "There's supposed to be a policeman here. Whenever beer's served on school property, a policeman's supposed to be present."

We finished our drinks and walked down to the lounge, speculating on the risks the university faced should someone stumble into the path of a streetcar or drive into the Mississippi on the way home.

I was in no mood for studying. Katie certainly wouldn't be studying—Loyola had Halloween off—so I called her to see if she wanted to go to a haunted house. It was something I had been promising for the past couple of weeks. She was all for it. I asked Jonathan to come along. He thought about it, then declined. Ordinarily, he said, he didn't mind being a third wheel, but with his recent breakup, he didn't feel like being reminded of it just yet.

We walked outside together and stood in front of the law school. The building looked magnificent in the faint floodlight: calm, stately, proud. I had enrolled at Tulane without visiting the campus, knowing little more about the school than its reputation. The morning when I first saw the school was like Christmas as a kid. It was a thrill. I hadn't felt that kind of thrill in years. I had trouble getting to sleep the night before. I was up at the crack of dawn. I remember sitting in the car in front of the building and urging Katie to look. It was fabulous: red brick with pillars, standing on a lot of bright green grass with shrubs by the entrance shaded by giant oaks. How nostalgic would I be years from now? How would I remember Landrow and his jokes, his black Corvette and his pizza party? How would I remember three years that were flying by in the blink of an eye? When I was frazzled with work, sitting behind a desk late into the night, would I remember a leisurely Friday afternoon listening to other law students play guitar and sing on the school patio? In the floodlight, the building looked truly impressive. I didn't mind standing there on the front walk receiving the casual glances of passers-by. I had all the time in the world.

"That was inappropriate of Muder to come down on Arny like that in class, don't you think?" Jonathan said, more a statement than a question.

"The classroom is no place for a fair fight," I had to admit. Although others had evidently seen an incident coming, what had happened that day in Pollution Control had caught me completely by surprise. *In Re:*, the law school newspaper, had come out with a letter criticizing Muder for using class time to encourage students to participate in a job fair for minority students interested in environmental law, and I had somehow missed it. My first hint of trouble was when Muder began class with an attack on an unnamed student, a student who, she said, had sought her out on numerous occasions to discuss other matters but who hadn't had the courtesy to check facts with her before going public with criticism. The more she spoke, the more incensed she seemed to become. These things have a way of getting around. There are people downtown who would love to get their hands on something like this. Then suddenly she was finished, ready to get on with class.

"May I respond," a student near the front asked. His name was Arny Peterson. I didn't know him well.

"After class," Muder said.

You could almost hear the crackle of electric sparks from the other students.

Muder reconsidered. "No, let's clear the air," she said. "After all, we are studying the Clean Air Act."

And Arny met resistance on each point. Each statement of his just seemed to straighten the nail for Muder's hammer, which dropped with driving force again and again.

"The whole thing," Jonathan said, "was about jobs. When people are poor and struggling, there's always trouble. People do things they might not otherwise do when their livelihood's at stake. Landrow beats that drum all the time: You put a guy on the stand and he's got a wife and kids, a mortgage and a car payment, and he'll say what he has to say. It's not necessarily lying. He may think he's telling the truth. He's just saying what he has to say."

The episode with Muder made me think, made me realize, I suppose, that all this talk about jobs was real, that things were really rough out there. Nobody seemed to have a job. There were people on Law Review without a job. Tommy didn't have a job. Jonathan didn't have a job, either. He said he had sixteen rejections posted on his refrigerator.

"I've been getting interviews with the bigger firms," he said. "I think I'm competing with people who're better qualified than I am."

He may have been right. He was probably in the top twenty percent of the class. He had gone to UCLA. He had spent some time in a traveling actor's group. And he was an Eagle Scout. People probably wanted to meet him. The acting background might have hinted at the ponytail, but such things don't appear on one's resume, so Jonathan went to one interview after another and the rejections would soon cover every appliance in his kitchen.

"I'm not interested in the big firms," I said. "I don't think I fit in there. I'm looking for a nice medium-sized law firm."

"I thought if worst came to worst, I could just take a public interest job. I didn't know that would be so difficult." He laughed.

"Isn't it funny. It's easier to find a job working to destroy the environment than find one keeping it clean. Is it a problem with the profession? the culture? or what?"

"A wise man once told me that the most important thing in life is the relationships we form with others. I thought that was pretty smart."

I thought it over.

"Of course," Jonathan added, "I was pretty drunk at the time."

"Yeah."

There was an awkward silence.

"How's your casenote?" I asked.

"I was late getting it in," he told me. "I was in the computer room putting the finishing touches on it. Nick Sutton was there working on something. I asked him if I could have some more time, and he said, 'No problem.'"

"That's cool."

"But when I gave it to him, he said something that bothered me."

"What?"

"Well ..."

"What did he say?"

"He said, 'Oh, I thought you were doing a comment.'"

"What's the problem with that?"

"I don't know. Just the way he said it."

"Your casenote has a good chance of getting published, at least."

"I don't know."

I told Jonathan about the interview I'd had with April Newton. "But don't say anything about it to Tommy," I cautioned him.

"Why?"

"Because he could've done the same thing," I said.

"I suppose that's right."

On the way to the haunted house, I asked Katie what a wise man looked like. Did he wear a beard? scraggly clothes? I pictured Jonathan in a poet's bar talking to a wise man. I used to go to poetry readings as an undergraduate. I remembered a young man reading about distant places. Young men always seemed to talk about distant places. I sat with my friends at the end of the bar near the back of the room. An old man near us shouted, "Ever been there?" We laughed. The poet continued: more lovers, more exotic ports. "Ever been there?" the old man cried. We laughed again. The bartender made the old man finish his coffee. I felt bad for encouraging him. Perhaps he was wise. I imagined that most wise men were old, single, alone, poor, sitting in bars drinking coffee. Now he was out in the cold. There was just a hint of snow in the air. I watched him through the window walking away, down the cold street, toward his own tropical island.

*   *   *

The next day, I received a letter from Branegan, Reed, Dowd & Spatz, one of the swankiest firms in Columbus:

> Dear Mr. Westphal:
>
> Your resume and letter dated October 11 were forwarded to me by Wendell Farmer who asked me to respond.
>
> Your application for a summer clerk position is still under consideration. In an effort to complete your file and assist us in our deliberations, please send copies of your law school transcript and references to Christine Forrest, our Manager of Professional Personnel, at your earliest convenience.
>
> We appreciate your interest in Branegan, Reed, Dowd & Spatz and look forward to hearing from you in the near future.
>
> Sincerely,
>
> Neil W. Benetton
>
> NWB/CAF/cak
> cc: Christine A. Forrest
> T. Wendell Farmer, Esq.

Branegan, Reed was a great firm, but I was hardly excited. It was more of a burden than a blessing, really. Getting a letter like that seemed just to prolong the agony. Now I had to send off a transcript and a letter listing references, which meant contacting people who would say something nice about me should Branegan, Reed inquire, should it matter, which it didn't. These giant firms string you out sometimes like a Chinese noodle. At least I had references at Simoneaux. I would have to contact Worth, though. He was, after all, my advisor. I thought I could just drop a note in his mailbox at school explaining the situation. Then I'd stop by after class in case he had any questions.

October 31
(Thursday)

Bubbles.

Assume an existing plant in an area is nonattainment—that is, an area not meeting the applicable air quality standards. It has two smoke-stacks and now it wants to add a third. It emits more than 100 tons of a pollutant, which means it is a major source and must meet Lowest Available Emissions Requirements ("LAER") and Reasonable Further Progress ("RFP"). What if the modification adds only 50 tons but the existing stacks emit greater than 100 tons of a pollutant? This is still a major source. What if the plant adds a third stack and eliminates the other two, emitting exactly the same amount of the pollutant? If there is zero addition, then the Clean Air Act imposes no further require-ments. The plant has "bubbled out of LAER-land." Cover a pile of waste with a blanket to reduce emissions? Fine … as long as there is zero addi-tion there are no new drills.

The bubble principle allows for economic expansion, but is it an appropriate policy? Environmentalists argued that the bubble concept allowed industries to buy the right to pollute, maintained the status quo, provided a disincentive to find new technology, and rewarded industry for doing what it should have been doing all along. Moreover, the EPA itself had earlier rejected the bubble concept. Nonetheless, the U.S. Supreme Court approved the bubble concept because it allowed sensible economic growth and least-cost pollution control. According to the Supreme Court, the EPA had maintained a "consistent interpre-tation of flexibility" regarding the use of "bubbles."

Environmentalists were outraged, but Congress evidently liked the bubble concept because it took no steps to do away with bubbles in the 1990 amendments to the Clean Water Act.

November 2
(Saturday)

On Saturday morning I attended an ELJ meeting for reconners. Reconners are people who reconstruct the article based on the versions produced by the two sub and citers, proofreaders and cite checkers. Betty had asked me to recon an article for the next issue.

We gathered in one of the classrooms on the second floor of the law school to receive assignments, and before long it was clear that some of the senior members were unhappy that more of the work wasn't going to new members. Tad Thompson confronted Betty and Trisha. "Wasn't the point of bringing in new people so that we wouldn't be loaded down with so much work this semester?"

Betty said, "The new members haven't had Bluebook training." It was an answer she had apparently given before. "The new members don't know the Bluebook. They'll get more work next semester."

Thompson wasn't accepting any of it. He made a noise of slight disgust.

*   *   *

Dear Kenneth:

Thank you for forwarding your resume to our office. Although you have fine credentials, we are not presently in a position to discuss employment opportunities with you.

Best of luck in your job search.

Very truly yours,
ALLEN WESTMAN & CHENEY

Theodore T. Kravitz
Hiring Partner

TTK/jsw

*   *   *

Dear Mr. Westphal:

Thank you for your recent letter and resume. Our firm interviews a significant number of second year law students every fall from a variety of law schools for the relatively few second year summer associate positions available.

Our Hiring Committee has reviewed your resume and has concluded that an interview at this time would not lead to an offer of a position as a summer associate for next summer.

We appreciate your interest in Horst, Kane & Trumbull and hope that you are successful in your search for a satisfying position.

Very truly yours,

Martha C. Chatwin
Director of Recruitment

MCC:wtb
00706aab.(2)

*   *   *

Dear Mr. Westphal:

Your October 11 correspondence to Lisa Lange of our office has been forwarded to me in my capacity as Chairman of the Recruiting Committee. Due to the large number of resumes received and the relatively small number of available positions, it is necessary to limit in-house interviews. We regret that we are unable to extend an invitation to you to visit our offices for an interview.

We appreciate your interest in the firm, and wish you success in your professional career.

Very truly yours,

Craig G. Farley

CGF:mac

November 4
(Monday)

I was experienced enough with interviews by now to be a bit insulted to find two people younger than I was waiting to speak with me at The Avenue Hotel. Associates, I thought. Associates out on a field trip. The girl was skinny and shy. She had a close group of friends in high school, and they gossiped ferociously. The boy had floppy hair and played football for his high school team. They lost as many games as they won. He had been popular. His hair style hadn't changed since.

The boy told me he had also clerked at Simoneaux and was interested in who I had worked with at the firm. I gave him a few names. He knew some of the people, thought he might have known some others. The atmosphere was friendly. They were making the most of their morning. The girl was taking notes. She stuck to questions about my resume.

The boy said, "I was at Simoneaux two summers ago … when the firm had all that trouble." They both looked for my reaction, and I smirked appropriately. No reason for undying loyalty.

"Was that really big news?" I asked.

"Everyone was talking about it," he said.

"It made the papers?"

"I don't think it made the papers."

"Even people in England got word," the girl said. "I have an aunt in London who called and asked about it."

This was a new slant: Law Firm Scandal Travels English-speaking World. We were having a jolly good time. Poor Simoneaux. Such a fine firm, such a sterling reputation, but two years before several of the partners had gotten too friendly with some of the office support staff. Some people were caught in the act. The secretaries involved were hustled off to work elsewhere, but not before they snuck back into the office and placed brownies on the desks of all the partners involved.

The interview then settled down to business. After a few more questions about my background, the girl wanted to know if I had any questions for them. Yes, as a matter of fact, I did. Early on I had decided that this interview I would try something different: I'd give the impression that I knew what being a lawyer was all about. Being a lawyer isn't about looking up the law, making a dashing argument, writing lucid prose; it's about keeping clients happy, bringing new clients into the firm, turning water into wine.

"Well, I'm curious," I began. "Let's say I have a friend who started a small company importing products he's having made in the Orient and selling them mail-order to office supply stores across the country. His father spent his life in the office furniture business and they saw they could make and sell a product cheaper than it was being sold before. And it's worked. They're making all kinds of money. I joke that he'll be the Les Wexner of office furniture. Now what if I brought him into your firm. What would you advise him? Who would meet with him? What could the firm do for him?" I looked at the girl.

"Good question," she said, turning to the boy.

I looked at the boy.

"He would probably want to meet with Mr. Sanderson," the boy said. "He's done business with clients in the Far East."

The girl liked this answer.

I waited for more.

"Mr. Sanderson would probably want to introduce him to clients similarly situated."

"That's interesting," I said.

"Oh, really?" the girl said.

"Yes," the boy said. "He does that a lot."

"What about such things as preparing trust funds, financial security, those kinds of things?" I asked. I hadn't thought the questions through very far.

"Oh, we've got people who can do all that. Mr. Burnham is very good at that sort of thing."

I nodded, doing my best to seem interested, although his answer had chugged along at a very low altitude. I didn't think he had the slightest idea what legal services might be needed for a fledgling importing business suddenly grossing two hundred thousand and growing. He had instilled in me no confidence whatsoever. I probably made a mistake by looking satisfied with what they had told me. I left the interview repeating how much I'd like to work for their firm. The only comforting thought was that when the kids discussed my interview later with one of the partners at the firm, the girl would bring up my question and the boy would repeat his lame answer. Then they would have to listen to the partner tell them at length, in detail, and with astonishing clarity how they should have responded, how they should respond the next time something like that came up.

November 5
(Tuesday)

"I hear Bradford & Bain is having trouble," Dad told me as I spoke with him one evening on the telephone.

"Really?" I wanted to hear more. Bradford was one of the Columbus firms I had visited before the start of the year, the firm where I had written my own rejection letter by professing an interest in insurance litigation.

"I hear they're laying off," Dad said.

"They're such a good firm."

"Things are tough."

After I hung up, I wondered why I had been so surprised. The firm hadn't been getting great publicity lately. A couple of years before several of the firm's attorneys went bust trying to make a killing with a chain of Drug City stores in Colorado. Recently, the firm had been dragged into court for its handling of a divorce action. And now that I thought about it, their offices were terribly cramped. What lawyer could work in that sweatshop, anyway?

November 6
(Wednesday)

The next day I received a phone call from Columbia Gas of Ohio. It was one of the secretaries in the Legal Department. She said that the hiring decisions were almost complete, my letter had reached them a little late, but I would still be considered if I could send a writing sample to them immediately.

"Can you act fast?" she wanted to know.

"I have a writing sample ready to go."

"Good."

"Does it matter if it's not on an environmental law topic? The paper I have is on ERISA."

"I don't … think so."

"I'll get it right out."

"Oh, one more thing. How did you get the name of Mr. Angle?"

"His name was included in a book of environmental attorneys," I told her, and thought better of it only after the words were out of my mouth.

> Dear Mr. Westphal:
>   Thank you for your interest in a summer position with Columbia Gas of Ohio.

At this time, I must inform you that all positions have been filled. However, I hope you will send us your resume next Fall. Thanks again for your interest.

Very truly yours,

Jerome Sharp Groner

JSG/lb

November 7
(Thursday)

Muder gave the class another of her not-so-hypothetical hypotheticals dealing with non-attainment Air Quality Control Regions. Baton Rouge was in deep trouble. It was non-attainment for ozone and carbon monoxide. The automobile was part of the problem. Industry in Baton Rouge was part of the problem. The publicly owned treatment plant was not in compliance. Beyond the sporadic bus service transporting less than two percent of the population, no public transportation system existed. The revised State Implementation Plan proposed emissions standards for automobiles, vehicle inspections, new boundaries for the Air Quality Control Region, as well as a new chemical facility ...

Different students were assigned various positions: EPA, Region VI, Dallas; City of Baton Rouge; Louisiana Chemical Association; American Automobile Association, Baton Rouge Chapter; and CLEAN, Citizens Longing for Environmental Attainment Now. The students sat at the front of the room ripping up and down various sections of the Code, looking for things that would make Muder nod her head or look up over the top of her reading glasses approvingly, perhaps even raise her hands in the air and repeat whatever had just been said.

Role-playing is one modern response to the "Socratic Method," the process of teaching where the professor guides students by questions, often focusing on one hapless student. The Socratic Method has been under attack for some time now. Poorly done, it is almost useless. In the wrong hands, as many have noted, it can become an instrument of terror. Ralph Nader purportedly called it "the game only one can play." Scott Turow observed that it could leave students with the ineradicable impression that it is somehow characteristically "legal" to be heartless, to be brutal. Any given semester at any law school, there's likely to be an editorial in the school newspaper decrying the Socratic Method as archaic. Professors, especially the younger ones, are sensitive to the criticism. Today, the quiet law student is less likely to be put in a position of ridicule—called on at random and pelted with questions—than at any time in recent history. Professors adopt other ways to foster class participation. Some professors have "experts" designated for a particular day or days during the semester. Others let students work in groups or make presentations or, as Muder did, assume various roles. Many use the seating chart only as a threat against complete apathy. Today the students most likely to be called upon are those who let the professors know, in one way or another, that they are open to the give-and-take of classroom discussion. The odd result is that a hand raised in the air is an invitation to spar, an invitation to be grilled.

Student: Well, I wanted to ask about …

Professor: Why don't you go ahead and answer my question.

(Laughter.)

It's happened too often not to notice.

The emphasis of young professors today is more on gentle persuasion than intimidation. These days, professors who come down hard on students risk student wrath supported by at least two decades of criticism, derisive student evaluations, and ramifications for tenure and salary increases. Law school today is, with little doubt, a kinder, gentler place than the experience simultaneously criticized and glorified by Scott Turow. In many ways, the softening of law school should be of little surprise given the disintegration in recent years of the mystique surrounding the legal profession—the attack on legalistic writing, the rebirth of legal advertising, the trend toward alternative dispute resolution, and, of course, the number of "tell all" books on the subject. Students today recognize that they are consumers of a product, and law schools with an ear to the complaints and an eye on the bottom line often accept the adage that the customer is always right. Today, students who go to law school expecting to find their absent father are amazed to find instead their mother passing out cookies on Fridays and cards on Valentine's Day, which is exactly what I found at Tulane.

*   *   *

After class, I found a note in my folder from my wife, Katie. Kimball Donilan, the recruiting coordinator at Gaines, had called. I was to call her back as soon as possible. If she wasn't at her desk, I was to have her paged. The phone number was scribbled on the note.

This was good. Gaines had called. They wanted me to call, have them paged. This was very good.

I went immediately to Career Services where two phones were set up to make long-distance job-related calls. I had seen students sitting there making "cold calls" by the hour. I called Katie first to see if Kimball had said anything more than was on the note. Katie couldn't add anything; Kimball had left the message on our answering machine.

Okay. It was three o'clock, four o'clock in Columbus. I dialed. Kimball wasn't at her desk, so I asked the receptionist to have her paged and waited.

"Hi, Ken," Kimball said. Her voice sounded far away. She must have been talking through a speaker phone, perhaps from the office of one of the lawyers at the firm.

"Hi, Kimball." I tried to sound confident and friendly.

"Here's what we're going to do," she said. "We'd like you to come in for an office visit."

Okay. It wasn't the offer I had been hoping for. After waiting so long for their response, I thought they might just make me an offer on the basis of what they already knew about me. After all, I had previously met with four or five members of the Recruiting Committee. I wasn't sure what would be served by an office visit. Perhaps it was another way to string me along, another way for me to make a mistake. Well, if that was the hoop I had to jump through, I was willing. If I was going to be a trained dog, I had better learn to jump. Now was as good a time as any.

They wanted me in Columbus for dinner and a morning of interviews on Tuesday. I could have dinner either Monday or Tuesday evening. I could make the arrangements. Kimball gave me the phone number of the firm's travel service. She wanted me to get back with her the next day about my plans, and I promised to get back with her in the morning.

Before calling the travel agent, there were things to consider, mainly my class schedule. I wanted to miss as few classes as possible. Being in Columbus for interviews Tuesday meant that I would miss Remedies and Pollution Control. I was most worried about missing Pollution Control, but I figured Katie could go and take notes. The big question was whether I would have dinner in Columbus on Monday or Tuesday. Dinner on Monday night meant missing Monday's classes. Dinner on Tuesday night meant missing Wednesday's classes. In the end, I decided to have dinner in Columbus Monday night. I would leave New Orleans Monday morning after Evidence, miss B.E., have dinner Monday night, interview on Tuesday, miss all of my Tuesday classes, and be back in New Orleans Tuesday night.

I began making calls.

*   *   *

That evening, I returned to school for a mandatory reconner meeting. I now had in my possession the article I would recon, a pile three inches thick with more than 200 footnotes, all held together by rubber bands. The article was written by Senator Conroy and titled "Behind the Scenes Banter: The Clean Air Act," basically a historical analysis of the passage of the Clean Air Act Amendments of 1990. Betty had left it in my folder with this message:

Here is Conroy. JUST to remind you:
1) Call your readers and tell them what to look for. Also, make sure they know & understand the typesetting symbols (you may have to meet with them).
2) Give them 1 galley copy and the manuscript
3) They have until Saturday A.M. (the exact time is up to you) to turn this in to you (it may say me on the memo)
4) You should make your readers' changes (as well as your own) on your CLEAN GALLEY PROOF and then turn all 3 things in (in my folder) by Tuesday 10:00 A.M.
Call me if you have any questions.
P.S.
—reread memo
—use red ink
—be neat

Madeline Fugh, another of the editors, distributed instructions on how to mark the pages for the typesetter. I tried to concentrate on what she said, but her words were often lost.

November 8
(Friday)

Landrow reiterated to the class his recommendation that we read first the Federal Rules of Evidence, then the advisory comments to the rules, then the textbook, a strategy he had mentioned the first week of class.

"I'm not reading the textbook," Jeremy Johnson told me after class. Jeremy sat next to me in class. He was an older student with an electrical engineering background and Procter & Gamble knocking at the door.

"Really?"

"I'm going to focus on the rules and class notes. I'll probably work some old tests."

"Focusing on class notes is always a good idea."

I knew what he was thinking by skipping the textbook. I hadn't been reading the assignments for several weeks. The book was simply verbose. Jeremy was right. The rules were the key and, of course, the class notes. Landrow had said the first day of class that the exam would be taken from the class notes. I decided I could afford to believe him. What clinched my decision was that Emanuel's Outlines had issued a new edition of Evidence that was organized in the same way Landrow was teaching the course. So I would study Emanuel's, review my class notes, and near exams, spend a day or so reading the rules to make sure I hadn't missed anything. Besides, Landrow didn't even seem to know what was in the textbook himself. Once when a student asked him a question he said, "Where'd you get that?"

"Right here in the textbook."

"Let me see that ... well ... that's pure nonsense."

Today Landrow was telling us about the interesting question of hearsay. A witness who observes a fact can report that fact. This is not hearsay because the witness's demeanor may be observed. However, if a second person observes some fact and relays it to another who reiterates it, the reiteration is hearsay. A telephone directory is hearsay that someone lives at a particular address. We should be careful to watch for hearsay within hearsay. For example, a police report is hearsay, and if the report contains the statement of a purported witness, the statement could be hearsay within hearsay. Unravel the mysteries with exceptions to exceptions. Get the evidence into court.

Get facts before the jury. Draw inferences from those facts. Keep the video tape of your story running ...

*　　　*　　　*

I was telling myself I could prepare for a closed book exam in exactly the same way I prepared for an open book exam—by reviewing as I normally would and making diagrams from my class notes to get an overview of the course. The only difference was that I would have to memorize my diagrams. But given the energy I was expending on things outside of class, the thought of two closed book exams was disturbing. Evidence was closed book, and that wouldn't change, so I had to keep working on Tarenzella. Halfway through the semester, with the issue still apparently unsettled, I typed a second note and put it in her mailbox:

> **Dear Ms. Tarenzella:**
> **Please consider making the final exam "open note." We are concerned that the "open statute" method of examination you have proposed may benefit the less upright students at the expense of those who obey the letter and spirit of the rule. Although students are bound by the Honor Code, the fact is that some students will abuse the opportunity to write in the margins of their statutes. Such a situation would be unfair to students who abide by the rule.**
> **Thank you very much for your consideration.**
> **Very truly yours,**
> **Concerned Students**

Tarenzella made no reference to this second note. By now, she was in a losing battle to cover the assigned material, becoming more and more shrill, lecturing more, and the more she lectured, the more she fell behind.

*   *   *

Canceled classes were not particularly unusual. It is common in law school for a professor to miss class. After making the effort to come to school, students typically grumble, especially near the end of the semester when make-up classes cram already busy days. But for the most part students have come to accept canceled law classes as a fact of life. For one thing, law professors often do consulting work on the side that takes them out of town. The more common reason, I began to suspect, was that a certain freedom of lifestyle was *quid pro quo* for smaller salaries. Exercise of their freedom was also a reaction to the life they once led practicing corporate law, a reaction to marking off their days in six-minute increments. Often I would see professors at Audubon Park on bicycles or in colorful jogging suits attempting to wring their new found freedom for every drop of sunshine and green grass they could impress upon their consciousness.

With the swelling ranks of day students and lawyers continuing their education at night, finding an empty classroom for make-up classes was tough to do at Tulane. Tarenzella had scheduled her make-up class for Friday at three o'clock. Students groaned and alleged the usual conflicts, but she finally stood firm.

Judging from the attendance, the conflicts seemed to have won out. The aisles looked as if someone had taken target practice. Those still standing looked wounded. Then I noticed one woman drinking beer out of a shiny red plastic cup. Where were they giving out beer? Why didn't I know about it? Was there a party on the patio? Friday afternoon, a dull class, that cold beer looked pretty good, a way to balance things out. Then Tommy sat down next to me with a beer in his hand.

"There's a Law Review party," he explained. "We tapped a keg to celebrate the publication of the first issue. We just got it back from the printer's."

I licked my lips.

"You want one?" he asked.

"Well ..."

"You can have one. They said we could bring friends."

"Sure."

Francis Penwell was also interested, and Tommy shuffled off for a round. Tarenzella came in at the appointed hour, shut the doors, and organized her papers on the podium. Tommy came in a minute later, wrinkling his brow innocently toward the podium, carrying two beers in large red cups. But Tarenzella was concerned with other matters. It looked as if one student had brought along her father.

"I see we have a new face," Tarenzella said. She was being pleasant. She smiled. I could see how she could be charming. "I couldn't help but notice.... Are you observing?"

"Yes," he said, "I'm just an observer." The young woman to his right shuffled papers.

Tarenzella went on with class. The empty seats convinced her to postpone the discussion on financial accounting and go over instead the economics of the firm, a section she hadn't planned on covering in class. Suddenly I realized what was perhaps the best reason to miss a make-up class: You don't miss that much. No professor wants to teach students one or two at a time during office hours for weeks on end. One way or another, professors usually find a way to cater to the absentees.

So Tarenzella spent the day discussing the most basic aspects of corporate management: risk-bearing, incentives, and monitoring. What should be the compensation structure of the corporation? What were the risks? What were the variables? Who was in control of the variables? How should the parties decide to allocate the risks? What factors were involved? How does a risk-averse person differ from a risk-avoiding person? Who bears the cost of the controllable risks? Who can best bear the risk?... There were the sorts of questions that occupied corporate management, the stuff of meetings and Total Quality Management and all other kinds of common sense the discussion of which keeps people in the executive suite busy. How to make the workers more productive. The U.S. shouldn't be making shoes, but we can't all be lawyers and executives. Can we? Perhaps we'll all be managers. How to best manage. How to get the most out of the workers? Carrot or stick? A little of both? Pass the donuts, please. We'll teleconference Thursday.

—Are we connected? Great. Give us your report. Take your time, Sam. Bill and Frank and Sara are here, too.

—Hi, Bill.

—Hi.

—Hi, Frank.

—Hello, Sam.

—Hi, Sara.

—How've you been, Sam?

—Great, just great.

—How'd you survive the storm down there?

—Say, the funniest thing happened ...

We finally decided the role of shareholders and managers in a corporate context relied on the separation of ownership and control.

How do we solve this tension?

Incentives and monitoring.

After class, Tommy offered to take me up to the Law Review offices for a refill. I quickly accepted, my chance, after months of wondering, to finally see where the school's elite spent their days.

The offices were on the top floor of the law school. As the door opened, I looked down a hallway that stretched the length of the building. On one side were perhaps twenty offices with windows to the outside world. At the end of the hall was the Law Review's private library, extensive enough to satisfy most medium-sized firms. Several sets of case reporters lined the shelves. Scattered about the room were sofas and reading chairs. In the corner, I recognized the editor, sitting at one of the computer terminals, typing furiously. He probably lived up here, I figured.

Tommy picked up a copy of the newest Law Review volume and showed me his name inside the front cover.

"Now you know you've accomplished something," I told him.

"I didn't do much work on this issue," he said. "Next issue'll be full of stuff I've worked on." He took the copy with him. He probably took another copy every time he walked through.

Back out in the hallway, we studied the photographs of past Law Review members hanging along the wall, noted the changing fashions and hairstyles. The best year was 1972. Ties were no longer essential, and, if worn at all, were thick and crazily patterned. The pictures had been taken outside. The hair was wild, the sideburns long. Within a few years, the effect was gone: the ties were back, the shirts white, the hair neat. Tommy wanted to show me what being editor-in-chief could do to a person. We looked at two pictures that showed how in the course of a year a man of 23 was left knocking on middle age. The after-effect was a bit shocking. The man's eyes were half-drawn. His hair had thinned. He looked like he had lost thirty pounds. No doubt bad photography played a part, but there was no denying that the poor fellow had emerged from his stint as the top person somewhat worse for the wear. Weary was the word. He had earned whatever rewards the title would later bring him in life.

Tommy and I had a good laugh.

I was interested in seeing the pictures of some of the partners at Simoneaux, Troy & Walters. Morton Jones, the person who had helped me get the job, had graduated in 1973, but most of the giants at the firm had graduated in the 1950s. In 1958, the top three people at Simoneaux, the people who really ran the firm, were all together on the Law Review staff, all roaming the hallowed hallway. Their images remained, frozen in youth with moistened hair. Ressner looked ready for a fight. Conklin had a certain gawkiness about him. He must be brilliant. Jackall, who was said to really run Simoneaux, looked even then like the big man on campus, much like a young John Updike.

At the other end of the hall, near the door, was the lounge. Inside, we found eight or ten people relaxed on sofas and chairs, drinking beer and eating pretzels and cheese from wooden bowls. The room had a television, refrigerator, microwave, and water cooler. The keg was on ice next to the sink. The Law Review was a big money maker. No doubt about that. Tommy filled our cups, and we went back up the hall to see where he worked.

The office itself was rather plain. I leaned against a metal desk that looked like it had been built with the building.

"Have you made any outlines yet?" I wondered, relaxing now.

"I'm in the process," he told me. "I hope this semester goes well.... I've been so darn busy."

"You're through with your Law Review stuff, though."

"For this semester. Next semester I have a comment to write."

"Are you going to work on it over Christmas?"

"I'd like to have it finished over Christmas. I'm going to rework the paper I wrote for the toxic torts seminar."

"Can you do that?"

"I'm going to. There's no way I'm going to write another."

"Maybe you should ask someone."

"They'll just say no. Marie Burnbaum asked the managing editor if she could rewrite a paper of hers and he said he didn't think so. I'm not going to ask."

"You just have to be careful, I suppose, that you don't violate any rule."

"I'll check," he said. "The paper won't be the same, though. I'm adding new sections. Really, I'm just building on some of the same research. There's no way I could start again completely from scratch."

"Just don't tell Marie Burnbaum."

"Did you know her husband's a partner at ... what's the firm Landrow works for?"

"Glennon, Moid. Her husband's a partner, huh?"

"A lot of people up here have connections, a father or husband, you'd be surprised. It's almost essential." He looked thoughtful. "People don't realize how many doors have already been shut. It all happens in the first year, the first semester, really. I didn't have a clue. My grades went up a lot during the second semester. I'm finally starting to get the hang of law school. But already there are doors that are shut."

"It'll help to have Law Review on your resume."

"Maybe, but if I'd known what some of these people knew the first year ..."

"Connections are important, I suppose, but that can't be the whole story. Knowing someone can tell you what to study, I suppose. I mean, there are at least three reasons why these people are successful. First, there's genetics. Some of these people are just plain smart. Second, having a parent or husband in the profession might give an extra incentive to succeed, maybe just that little extra effort to please, you know, to be accepted or just to feel good about themselves. Third, you're right of course, having someone in the family is always a big help when it comes to stuff like making outlines. I know a girl whose father corrected her outlines. I'm still not sure how to make a good outline."

"Her father's a lawyer?"

"Uh-huh."

We walked back down the long hallway, a barrel of a gun, and I was being shot back out into the real world. I told Tommy that soon his picture would be on the wall like all of the others, soon he would be frozen in time, a bemused expression on his face. My last glimpse of the Law Review offices was a sign stuck to the back of the door, clearly a response to the tee shirts many were wearing urging people to "make love, not law review." The sign, a piece of cardboard with neatly printed letters, offered the Law Review's alternative:

MAKE LOVE TO LAW REVIEW.

*   *   *

Dear Mr. Westphal:

Thank you for expressing an interest in a summer law clerk's position here at Sabina, Kohr & Land. At this time we are not hiring for this position. However, we will keep your resume on file if our situation changes.

Very truly yours,

Sarah Krantz

SK/mkf

*   *   *

Dear Mr. Westphal:

This will acknowledge your recent correspondence. We regret to advise that, at the present time, we anticipate no openings in our law firm.

We do, however, wish you the best of luck in your legal career.

Yours very truly,
FREDERICK, CAIN, COY &
SPERLING

Richard B. Coy

*   *   *

Dear Mr. Westphal:

Thank you for sending your resume to us recently. While your credentials are impressive, we do not have any positions available at our firm at this time. However, we will keep your resume on file in case our situation changes. In that event, we will contact you for an interview.

Thank you for your interest in our firm.

> Very truly yours,
> JACKSON, ARCHIBALD &
> GRIFFIN
>
> F. Scott Archibald, III

FSA:kt

*   *   *

Dear Mr. Westphal:

We are in receipt of your resume with respect to a summer clerkship with our firm. Please be advised that this office hires for year-round positions as opposed to strictly summer assignments.

Thank you for your interest in our firm. We are certain that you will be successful in your legal endeavors.

> Very truly yours,
> QUISENBERRY, COYLE &
> ROGERS
>
> Daniel A. Quisenberry
> Administrator

DAQ/plb

Others may very well have had their secretaries sign these letters, but this last was the only one I had noticed with a rubber stamp.

11

The Conroy article was supposed to be back in my folder by Saturday so I would have time to make changes and return it to Betty by Tuesday. But the article wasn't in my folder Saturday. It wasn't there Sunday. It wasn't there Monday when I checked before Evidence. I gave Francis Penwell, the sub and citer on the article, as much latitude as possible. People spoke highly of his work. He probably should have been an associate editor, so I resisted pulling rank. Saturday hadn't bothered me. Sunday I made a special trip to the school. By Monday I had to say something. I caught him on the way out of Evidence class.

He turned slowly.

"Did you finish the article?" I asked him.

"I finished it Saturday," he said. "I put it in Betty's folder."

"You put it in Betty's folder?" The paper had been sitting in Betty's folder since Saturday? Betty may have picked it up? She may have assumed it was completed?

"That's what the instructions said to do," he said.

"Okay."

I ran down the stairs. Betty's folder was empty, so I wrote her a note referring to a mix-up and promising that if she gave me the article again, I'd return it to her by Wednesday. A day late, I thought, but probably okay. I would worry about it when I got back from Ohio. There went Wednesday morning. Once again, B.E. would suffer. But just then I didn't have time to worry. Before I could leave for the airport, I had to get home, pack, make copies of my ERISA casenote should anyone ask for a writing sample, and make sure Katie would cover Pollution Control in my absence.

(5:21 p.m. EST)

Touchdown. Columbus, Ohio.

It was cold when I got off the plane. I was back in the Midwest. Because I knew I'd have no time to change before dinner, I stepped off the plane in suit and overcoat. My parents and my sister Janice were waiting. After we retrieved my bags, I went into one of the restrooms and put in my contact lenses.

(6:32 p.m. EST)

Dinner was at the Overlook Restaurant, atop one of the larger office buildings in downtown Columbus. I dined with Ivan Mayle, Carl Leavy, and their wives. Ivan Mayle, I knew, was on the firm's Hiring Committee. Carl Leavy was a new hire, a lateral who specialized in environmental law. He was a graduate of Michigan, as were a number of members of the firm.

Ivan ordered wine. His wife talked about her children, their house in the woods, the animals that appeared occasionally on their back porch, sometimes startlingly large animals. Carl talked about his fishing boat. The questions came slowly, between courses, the mood carefully casual. We sat looking at each other and at the view of Columbus at night, the cars in the distance forming lines of lights heading home.

November 12
(Tuesday)
(10:00 a.m. EST)

I was standing in the lobby of Gaines, Duncan, Duffy & Gray at precisely ten o'clock. Kimball was waiting for me with Carrie Knowlton, one of the firm's young associates, my first interview of the day. Carrie was a good choice, I thought. We had both studied English at Ohio State and knew a number of the same people. I was happy to see she had received an offer. The firm had really tested her during her clerkship the previous summer. I would see her sitting at her desk dictating a memo one minute and running errands for Mr. Gaines the next. Although she had the credentials—managing editor of the Ohio State Law Review—I doubted her chances when she didn't take part in the mock trial at the end of the summer. But here she was, leading me up the stairs to her office where, shortly after the interview began, I asked her if she still wrote poetry, and she told me she didn't really have time for that anymore.

In quick succession, I met a young associate out of the University of Virginia who had just run a marathon, a woman who had clerked for the federal judge overseeing the Pete Rose gambling decision, and a public utilities lawyer with an interest in movies. The public utilities lawyer had a big toothy grin. He asked me who my next interview was with. I told him Mr. Duncan.

"He plays it prim and proper around the office," he told me. "He takes his role as representative of the firm seriously, but he can loosen up after hours."

My interview with Mr. Duncan would be one of the more important interviews of the day. He was the name partner on my dance card, the man with the large corner office. His opinion would weigh heavily on my chances. He may run around at firm retreats with a drink in his hand and his tie wrapped around his head, but his name was on the door.

"You want to work for a law firm, do you, Kenneth?" he asked when I took my seat. From where I sat, on the edge of the building against the glass, it looked as if one misstep and I'd tumble twelve floors to the pavement.

"I want to start with a law firm."

"You want to *start* with a law firm."

I nodded. This was no deadly admission. Working for a law firm is a good way to keep options open for the future, a smooth stepping stone to corporate law, public service, or a government job, and a government job leads, if anywhere, back to law firms because law firms pay better. I wanted to start with a law firm. Everybody has some connection that might lead to a legal job, a friend, a friend of a friend, an uncle, something, someone, somewhere, somehow, and this was where my connection led, to this firm, this chair in this corner office talking to this partner. I just wanted a break. "I want to start with a law firm," I said. I wanted to start with Gaines.

Mr. Duncan looked back at my resume. Mr. Barrett Duncan. He was, I thought, a likable fellow. Businesslike, to be sure. On his head was a nice mound of fluffy white hair, his face worn but handsome, and he occasionally highlighted a tired expression by rubbing his eyes as if he couldn't believe the things people tried to pull.

He wanted to know why I had gone to Tulane. That's what everyone wanted to know: Why Tulane? Why? I don't know. It sounded like fun. A few weeks ago I might have stumbled on the question. Why not Ohio State? Why pay so much in tuition? Why go so far away if you want to work in Ohio? Why forego a lifetime of professional contacts, the chance to work for a prospective employer during your third year of school, the advantages of studying nearer to home? Why? Good questions. Now I was able to describe Tulane's environmental law program and still make it clear that I wanted to return to Columbus after graduation. New Orleans was a fun place to visit, but my family was here.

"I am the eldest of five children," I told him, a fact I mentioned too infrequently during interviews. "We've all stayed in the Columbus area. I look forward to coming back."

"What does your uncle do?"

"He works for Brack Enterprises."

"Is he on the Board?"

"He's president of Brackensack Manufacturing, one of its subsidiaries."

"He works with Daniel Barnes."

"Yes, that's right."

Daniel Barnes was my uncle's boss. There were always bigger fish; he didn't have to tell me that. But I didn't have to remind him Brackensack was too big to throw back.

(11:48 a.m. EST)

When both of the associates I was to eat lunch with were held up momentarily on business, I had time to poke my head in the library to say hello to MaryAnne, a friend from two years before when I worked with her in the library and ran errands for the firm. I found her at her desk, sorting mail and magazines. Nothing had changed. Piles were stacked across her desk and on the floor. We had just started to talk when Dwight Montgomery, a friend from elementary school, appeared in the doorway.

"I saw you in the hall," he said. "I figured you were interviewing." He pointed a finger at his temple, making me laugh along with him. He figured things out, all right. How strange it was to see Dwight again. He had been practicing law now for almost four years, having gone straight to law school after college. Somehow he had landed a job at the venerable Branegan, Reed, Dowd & Spatz. He had impressed someone. He was a likable person, I suppose. That went a long way.

"You working on a project with Gaines?" I asked.

"I work here now," he said.

Here? What happened to Branegan, Reed?

He must have read my expression. "I like it a lot better than Branegan," he said.

Dwight made everything simple. Well, yes, of course, if you like it better here, then by all means…. MaryAnne was looking at him with admiration.

"I wish you were on the Recruiting Committee," I said.

He laughed, thought about saying something, thought better of it. I wondered whether it would have done me any good. I wasn't sure. We had not seen each other much in recent years.

"You don't look so good," MaryAnne said.

"I'm sick," I said, meaning that I hadn't felt well all morning.

"I'm in bankruptcy," Dwight volunteered. He meant that others were in bankruptcy and he was paid to make sure they got out of it with their house and two cars.

I nodded. I knew that. I had recently looked him up in Martindale-Hubbell. Perhaps he thought the fact that he was in the bankruptcy section would make me feel better, that I might not like the idea of taking assignments from him. I didn't, not at all, but that could be avoided.

Dwight had backed up and was standing in the hallway, looking one way and then the other. I grabbed his hand and said I hoped to see him next summer, that I was late for lunch. He nodded and shuffled off to his office.

(12:04 a.m. EST)

One of the associates, Phil Hillenbrand, was waiting for me in the lobby when I came down the steps. Allen Dowd was still in a meeting; he would meet us in the restaurant. It was right downstairs.

Phil was about my age. The first thing he asked me, before we stepped onto the elevator, was why I wanted to work at Gaines. His token interview question. Apparently, he viewed the whole interview process, certainly his role in the selection of summer associates, with amusement, a slight grin that seemed to complement his designer suit, his cufflinks, his stiff hair.

"The people," I told him. It was a note I had been chiming all morning: A law firm is nothing but the people who make it up. I worked here a couple of years ago. I know the people, like the people, get along with the people.

We followed a hostess to our table. As we walked, I looked around to see what people were eating. Mostly pasta dishes, I decided. Mr. Gaines saw us first. We were being lead right past his table. "Well," he said, his hand rising to greet me. I shook it and gave my best smile.

"Nice to see you again," I said. Phil hadn't stopped. I shook Mr. Gaines' hand and moved along as well.

"Nice to see you," Mr. Gaines said over my shoulder, his voice resonant, the sound of breaking wood.

Moving along had been instinctual. Mr. Gaines would only have said something to make me feel comfortable, something appropriate and mildly amusing, something that would have left me standing beside his table searching for a rejoinder and finding only a hollow chuckle.

Mr. Gaines had started the firm, I once figured, when he was in his early thirties, not much older than I was. We didn't have much in common. I was hardly a younger version of himself. I certainly respected him, though, and would have liked to study him more closely. He struck an impressive figure. Tall with wavy hair, he dressed impeccably and moved with speed and grace. In legal parlance, he was what is known as a "rainmaker," someone who can bring in the big clients. He was responsible for bringing my uncle's business to the firm. Under his leadership, the firm had enjoyed steady growth over the past two decades. Mr. Gaines was also somewhat rare among lawyers these days in that he could claim to practice in all areas of law. Of course, as one of the associates told me, it helped that he surrounded himself with good people.

Mr. Gaines.

I smiled and kept moving.

"It was nice to see Mr. Gaines again," I told Phil as I took my seat. "I was glad to have the chance to say hello."

"He's paying for the meal," Phil said.

Allen Dowd joined us a few minutes later, and we placed our orders. I ordered pasta, the house specialty. Not too expensive. Easy to eat. Allen made no secret that he hadn't looked over my resume before our meeting, and we began lunch with him nibbling a little at his cheeseburger and a little at the edges of my life. Soon he set my resume aside altogether.

"What was the most significant event in your life?" he asked. He got both hands on his burger. The meat looked burned. I knew when he ordered it well done that it would come back black.

"I'm not sure I ever thought about that," I admitted.

Where was my life going and why? Pinpoint the course of your life to one moment in time ...

"I supposed it was coming across some of the books I did in high school," I said. Not bad. After all, I had gone on to study journalism and English. Something had pushed me there. "Jack Kerouac, Herman Hesse, Kurt Vonnegut ..."

"Kurt Vonnegut is my favorite author," he said. "What books do you like?"

"Oh, what did I read? What is it, *Slaughterhouse Five*?"

"About the fire bombing of Dresden?" he said.

"Yes. It was made into a very good movie. People didn't think it could be done. I think it won some awards at Cannes."

"I'll have to rent it," he said.

I had the floor. Books. What books had I read in high school? What other authors did I like? I started to talk about James Agee. I had written my master's thesis on Agee's *Let Us Now Praise Famous Men*, a book part biography, part documentary, part sociology, part religious revelation. Agee had been working as a reporter at *Fortune* magazine during the height of the Great Depression when he and Walker Evans, the photographer, were assigned to go to Alabama to document the lives of people driven into the dust by difficult times. Agee lived with a family of tenant farmers, slept in their beds, ate their food, gloried in and raged at their condition.

I could talk about the strange publishing history of the book and its awkward place on the edges of the American Canon for hours. I was giving my opinion of the book's essential argument before I realized what I was doing. I had gone on a bit too long. I just stopped. Allen was looking at me. Phil was looking at his food.

"It's a great book," I said.

Allen turned to Phil. "How's your food?" he asked.

Rude, I suppose, but I was relieved to have the subject changed. Phil said he had been eating at one of the nicer restaurants in town and was served by a waiter with lesions on his arms, and Allen wouldn't rest until he knew the name of the restaurant. Our plates were taken away by a waiter with long sleeves, and Allen turned back to me.

"I always like to ask people to describe themselves in one word," he said.

That was one way to keep me from rambling. One word. This would be my comeback. One word. Wasn't it conventional wisdom to say your biggest weakness was that you worked too hard?

"Hard-working, I suppose," I said.

"Is that two words?" He looked to Phil and to me for a reaction. I smiled. Still, I wasn't thinking fast enough.

"A hard-working person," I said, almost mumbling. Then I had a thought. "No, I would say curious. That's the word I would choose— *curious.*" I liked that word. Being curious was a power word. Einstein lamented that too many people lost their curiosity as they got older. The important thing was to ask questions. Being curious was one of the keys to success, and I actually thought of myself as being curious.

"Why do you want to work at Gaines?" he asked.

I took a breath, glanced at Phil.

"The people," I told him. "I worked here a couple of years ago, and I like the people. I got along with everyone I worked with. I know Dwight Montgomery. We went to grade school together."

"That counts against you," he said, looking again at my resume.

I snickered appropriately. Phil gave me his grin. Somehow, Dwight had covered his backside coming out of Branegan, Reed. They probably never even asked about his grades. He had experience at one of the top firms in the state. He had the looks, the personality. I imagined he was announced to the people at Gaines with much fanfare. *That says something about our firm that we get people like Dwight, with the opportunities he had at Branegan*. With that start, he couldn't lose. He was one of the fiercest competitors I had ever known. Now he was captain of the firm basketball team, and Allen was still missing lay-ups.

In the elevator on the way back up to the office, I realized, with some pleasure, that I was taller than Allen by a head, at least it seemed that much as he leaned against the elevator wall. He had warmed up to me considerably. Now he was telling me, the more he thought about it, that, yes, *curious* was a good word. All the way back to the office: "Curious, yeah, that's a good word."

(12:58 p.m. EST)

After lunch, Phil made his excuses and returned to work. Allen escorted me to my next interview.

"It's too bad I won't get a chance to see Mr. Weiss," I said as we walked along. Sam Weiss was the head of the firm's Recruiting Committee. "I didn't see him on my itinerary."

"You know Sam Weiss?"

"Not well," I said. "When I worked here summer before last, I had the chance to run some papers up to Indiana for him. You should've seen the clunker I was driving."

Allen nodded. We turned around. He led me to the closed office door of Sam Weiss, knocked once, cracked the door, and we were welcomed.

Sam sat behind a desk stacked with papers, fountain pen in hand. He set it down and leaned back in his chair, waving us to take a seat.

"I just wanted to stop by for a moment and say hello," I said. "I was telling Allen how I'd run some court papers to Indiana for you summer before last."

"That case turned out very well," he said. "As a matter of fact, it was just decided."

I was happy to hear it.

"You're at Tulane, aren't you?"

"That's right. I understand you've been down there yourself, to New Orleans, I mean. My uncle said you argued a case before the Fifth Circuit for them."

"Have you ever been inside the Fifth Circuit?"

"Yes."

"The courtroom—"

"Oh, not the courtroom. I was thinking of the Fifth Circuit library."

"Oh, you should go just to see it. It's beautiful. The bench and the witness boxes are set up high. The wood paneling is gorgeous." He made as if he were touching the walls. I could see it, too, dark glossy wood, thick and strong, soft leather-cushioned chairs, high benches. Authority. Power. Prestige.

"Well, I heard the case went well," I told him. I explained that I was probably throwing a wrench in the careful schedule Kimball had set up, but that I just wanted to stick my head in and say "hello." And with that, Allen and I set out again, a little late now, to find Thomas Brown, my next interview.

Thomas Brown, it turned out, was nowhere to be found. Allen got on the phone and tried to find him. He had him paged. He called Kimball. Allen was very apologetic, and wouldn't go back to work until I was in good hands.

"Well," I said, "you can tell me a little more about yourself while we're waiting. What do you do for fun?"

"You mean aside from work?" he asked.

"Yeah," I said. "Aside from work."

"I lift weights," he told me. "I go down to the gym at lunch."

He looked like he probably lifted weights. How was I supposed to respond? I simply nodded, taking the warning he was giving the world at large.

I decided later I'd probably have to come up with an interest in weights somewhere down the road. A lot of people in the executive suite probably worked out. I often thought that physical strength could be an asset, even in the boardroom. One never knew when things would come to fisticuffs. Sometimes physical threats were the only way to get things done. The best offense is a good defense. In a game that was often strength of wills, a little edge could mean the whole difference.

I was starting to think that much in law had to do with endurance. Sitting in class is certainly one example, keeping one's mind from wandering for an hour and fifteen minutes at a stretch. So are exams: three hours of mental and physical endurance. So is law school: three years of sacrifices, three years of training to look for what can go wrong, of seeing how easily others have messed up their lives and wondering seriously about one's own. These interviews, though, were starting to wear me to a fine point and there was a real risk that I would break. Twenty minutes at a time focusing on every nuance, every nod of the head, wondering what a partner meant by a particular question, what an associate might have been thinking, what impressions might be drawn from my reactions, what I should ask next, how what I said in one interview would compare with what I said in another, whether the recruiting coordinator was listening over the intercom, whether I would have an umbrella if it were raining at noon, whether it is best to order something different from everyone else and appear independent or to order the same thing and convey camaraderie.... The whole process was wearying, and thinking too much about it, like thinking too much about anything, could be deadly.

(1:24 p.m. EST)

Thomas Brown had been called out of the office and didn't make it back for my interview. By the time we figured out where he was, though, it was time for my next interview, with David Washburn, the head of the firm's litigation department. I was looking forward to my interview with Mr. Washburn. On the plane, I'd had a chance to review the biographies of the members of the firm. Mr. Washburn had an interesting background. In law school, he had won first place in a national moot court competition. After graduating, he clerked for a federal court justice. Recently he had published a well-received series of articles on trends in toxic tort litigation. When I was working in the firm's library he had floated around a copy of a $6 million settlement check he had negotiated.

Mr. Washburn asked me a few of the traditional interview questions. I told him if I accomplished half as much my first five years out of law school as he had, I would be doing pretty well. I found myself telling him how I had sent my casenote to April Newton and ended up meeting with her. I gave him a copy I was carrying. He seemed interested.

Mr. Washburn insisted on walking me to my next interview, with Laurence Elson, a young-looking lawyer with thick glasses. I liked Laurence immediately. He had to be brilliant, I figured, because he didn't look like every other lawyer you meet. He even seemed a little nervous at the start of the interview.

After talking with him briefly about his practice area, labor law, I asked him a series of questions about his life away from work. I suppose I had an advantage over others who interviewed at the firm. While others would have to spend most of the interview getting through the basic questions about the firm's practice, about a particular attorney's area of expertise, about the clerkship program, I could focus on getting to know the person better. I asked Laurence where he lived and what he did in his spare time. He answered readily, and as he told me how he walked to work and considered himself a "news junkie," it occurred to me that everyone should ask these types of questions. Not only was I finding things we might have in common, some basis for a friendship, but also I was learning a great deal about the firm and the quality of life of its attorneys—how much spare time an associate has, how secure he feels about his job or his chances for advancement.

"You're interested in environmental law?" he asked me.

"That's right," I said. "Well, of course, I'm on the Environmental Law Journal."

"You're on the Environmental Law Journal?" he asked. He moved to make a notation on my resume, and looked to me again for confirmation.

"Isn't it on the resume?" I asked.

He looked again. "No."

"Oh, you have the old version," I said. "I've written onto the Environmental Law Journal since then. I'm now associate editor. Kimball should have given you the new copy." I tried to make light of it, but I felt betrayed. For some reason, Kimball had failed to circulate my most recent resume. Although I had worked at the firm before, many of these people I was meeting for the first time. The only impression they had of me before I walked into their office was what they could glean from my resume. What I said would be taken in conjunction with the words on the page. *Can't see how Mr. Westphal would be an asset to our Environmental Law Section.* How they evaluated me once I left their office would be affected by the impression they had already formed. *Not quite Gaines material.* Mr. Duncan had been surprised by my interest in environmental law. When I said, well, of course, I'm interested in environmental law, he took aim at my liberal arts background. "I'm not sure it's necessary," I had told him, struggling to hold on. I'm pursuing a certificate in environmental studies. I'm on the Environmental Law Journal. For goodness' sake, I'll know something about environmental law by the time I graduate.... But he didn't have a clue. To him, I was just another student who professed an interest in environmental law because it was a "hot" practice area. Who did these people think they were dealing with? What kind of favor did they think they were being asked to do? All of the effort I had made to write onto the ELJ, the classes I was missing now to interview, the time taken to travel back to Columbus, the stress of one interview after another … all for nothing. The punching I had taken at lunch suddenly made a little more sense. How could anyone take me seriously? How could I expect to land a job that most law students in the country would be delighted to have, a job that stressed quality of life and made sure of it by paying more than a thousand dollars a week to start?

"I'm interested in environmental law," I told Laurence. "That's one of the reasons I went to Tulane. They have a good program in environmental law, largely because of all the pollution problems down there. It's called cancer alley between Baton Rouge and New Orleans. No one drinks the water from the tap."

"You can't trust bottled water up here," he said. "There's no regulation on labeling. They can call it 'Clear Mountain Stream' if they want to."

"I hope there are some regulations in Louisiana. The tap water comes from the Mississippi, and who knows what's in it? Tulane has a very good program in environmental law. It offers a certificate in environmental law studies. You take a number of designated courses, administrative law, natural resources. Right now, I'm taking Pollution Control. We're studying the Clean Water Act, RCRA, CERCLA, that sort of thing."

"What does CERCLA stand for?" he asked.

And right then … I couldn't remember. The question knocked the answer right out of my head. Gone. The retrieval system had overloaded. The screen was blank.

"All environmental law is alphabet soup," I said, attempting to wave off his question. "There's MACT and BACT and BART." These were technical standards to the Clean Water Act, the only acronyms to pop into my head. What I was saying was true—environmental law was alphabet soup—but I had hardly given an answer to a straightforward question.

He changed the subject, and I refused to worry about it. He could ask Carl Leavy, the firm's environmental lawyer, what CERCLA stood for. Let's see if he could think of it right off the top of his head. Everyone just called it CERCLA or Superfund. Of course, as soon as I walked out of his office, I thought, Comprehensive Environmental Response Compensation and Liability Act. But no one called it that.

Still, I had to admit it was a clever question, even if he was just being curious. In a profession where appearances are almost as important as substance, perhaps knowing what CERCLA stands for is as important as knowing how the statute works.

(2:48 p.m. EST)

I looked forward to my interview with James Cole. The projects I had done for him during my stint at the firm had turned out quite well. I wanted to make sure, though, that he had my most recent resume.

He looked at the paper in his hand. "Yes," he said. "Here, it says right on the top: new resume." He pointed to the top of the page.

I relaxed, smiled.

"I reviewed it again just a few minutes ago," he said. "It was even more impressive than I remembered."

It turned out to be a good interview. My only goal was to bring up the work I had done for him, which I did right off. He had assigned me to the task of figuring out what attorneys at various firms around town were charging. Gaines didn't want to be the cheapest firm. It didn't want to be the most expensive, either. The fees charged by lawyers filing bankruptcy cases are public record, so the only trick was putting the information onto a useful chart to show how billing rates varied depending on the experience of the attorney and the size and rating of the firm. I found an attorney at Jones, Day, Reavis & Pogue with three years experience billing at $180 an hour. If, as is generally understood, one-third of an associate's billing goes toward firm expenses, one-third goes to the partners, and the final third makes up the associate's salary, then this associate was taking home $60 an hour, roughly $120,000 a year three years out of school. Not bad work if you could get it. Of course, there was no way he was billing all of his clients $180 an hour. That was reserved for big bankrupt corporations no longer watching the bottom line.

"Perhaps the most important thing I learned this summer," I found myself telling Mr. Cole, "is that you've got to make sure you're doing what the assigning attorney wants you to do. Not that I made any big mistakes, but I certainly avoided some potential ones by keeping the lines of communication open." He was listening. "I figure it's a lot like the relationship an attorney has with a client. You've got to know exactly what the client wants. You've got to keep the lines of communication open."

"That's right," he said. "I got a call the other day from a client who makes these pull toys, and he wanted to sell these pull toys. So he called me and we talked about a contract. About a week later it occurred to me that he needed the contract by such and such a date, so I prepared a contract and faxed it to him to reach him by the deadline. Then I got a call from him that he just wanted an estimate on the cost of the contract. I said, well, if you use the contract, you can pay me this. I suppose he could use the contract and I'd never know.... But you're right, you've got to know exactly what the client wants."

This was extraordinary talk from an interviewer, from a lawyer, period, because in rapid order lawyers become masters at covering their mistakes, captains of confidence. How we went from pull toys to Bob Greene, the newspaper columnist, I'm not sure, but we had a nice talk about some of his columns. Greene struck Mr. Cole as the sort of fellow one could just pop in on for a visit. He had thought about visiting Bob Greene once when he was in Chicago on business.

"He's Everyman," I suggested.

Mr. Cole liked that explanation: Everyman.

(3:23 p.m. EST)

My last interview was with Sheila White, a new associate at the firm. She hadn't been given the new resume, and I spent the initial part of the interview educating her. I also mentioned that I had gone to school with Dwight. She liked Dwight. She seemed to like me. I told her I couldn't believe it was getting dark outside already.

"It's depressing," she said.

Kimball was standing beside her desk when we returned. She didn't seem to know how to wrap up the day. There was an awkward silence. "Would you like a firm brochure?" she asked, pointing to the box of green folders next to her desk.

"No, thanks. I already have one."

"Oh."

"What happens next?" I asked.

The Recruiting Committee would be meeting the following week, she told me, and I would probably hear shortly thereafter. Final decisions would be made over the next several weeks. I wanted a list of people I had interviewed with, and she offered me a seat. She pulled my itinerary from her top drawer, crossed off the name of Mr. Brown. The list would make sure I didn't make any mistakes when I got around to writing the "thank you" letters. I didn't want to forget anyone.

"Carl saw the copy of the Environmental Law Journal you sent," she said.

"Yeah?"

"It's too bad there were no articles of yours," she said. "It didn't have your name in it."

"No, but the next one will," I told her. "I'm now associate editor." It was a point I wanted to make. She hadn't merely deprived me of membership on the ELJ, she had deprived me of my leadership position and cut off any conversation about my climb. My major law school accomplishment had been obliterated. My stepladder to the golden door had been stolen away.

"We might subscribe," she said. She had that look of resignation common to people who work with lawyers.

"We're certainly trying to get our subscription base up," I told her. "I have a friend on Law Review, and he took me up to their offices last week. It's like a penthouse suite up there. They have their own library. They have a lounge, refrigerator, microwave. They each have offices … about this size. They're big. It's like a country club or a fraternity. When I saw those offices I finally understood the affinity law review people have for one another, how important it is to be on law review."

I had said what I wanted to say. It was time to go. As she helped me with my overcoat, she mentioned that she had my writing sample.

"I wrote it for the Law Review write-on competition," I told her.

"Did you tell David Washburn that?"

I paused to think. It was a strange question. Had I left the wrong impression with Mr. Washburn? "I think so," I said.

Kimball seemed satisfied.

I apologized for the poor copy quality. "I know how important appearances are."

"At least you didn't typeset it," she said.

I laughed.

She had mastered, I decided, that look of resignation.

(7:40 p.m. EST)

Liftoff.

I opened the *New York Times* and read about a multi-millionaire who was giving up all his wealth, his businesses, the buildings, homes, helicopters, ranches, all of it in an effort, he said, to easier pass through the eye of a needle. After years surrounded by all the trappings of wealth, he was now distributing, disbursing, removing, reducing in size.

(11:42 p.m.)

Touchdown. New Orleans, Louisiana.

Katie didn't tell me in so many words that she had skipped Muder's class. Instead, she met me with the news that Jonathan had brought over a copy of his class notes. "He thought you were sick," she said.

"He knew I was interviewing."

"I told him that, and he said he remembered you saying something about it."

"Why didn't you go?" I asked. I knew the answer. She was afraid to go. She thought she would stand out. Muder called on people by sight. If she accidentally looked up, she might be singled out. If Muder didn't recognize a face, Muder would have all the more reason for calling on her. There were all kinds of terrible scenarios that ended up with Katie the focus of a hundred pair of eyes.

"You have Jonathan's notes," she said.

"Jonathan hardly takes notes."

"He brought over four pages of notes. They're on your desk."

Well, perhaps four pages of notes would be enough. I could figure out most of what I had missed. Of course, I was at the mercy of Jonathan, what he thought was important, what he felt like writing down. I added his notes to mine. I would look at them more closely later.

I went through the mail that had gathered while I was away:

> Dear Mr. Westphal:
>
> Thank you for your letter regarding summer employment with Battelle. Although it is too soon to say whether we will need a summer intern, we will keep you in mind if a position is available. Best of luck with your career.

Sincerely,

Barbara T. Rose
Senior Attorney

BTR:lat

*   *   *

Dear Mr. Westphal:

Thank you for your letter of October 25 directed to Brian T. Kelly inquiring about a Summer Associate position in environmental law with our firm.

While I believe that all our summer positions have been filled, I will forward your resume to the appropriate attorney in our firm for consideration. I wish you the best of luck in your search for a position.

Very truly yours,

David S. Abrams

DSA:eaw:1685q

November 13
(Wednesday)
(9:05 a.m.)

The next morning, I was sitting in the student lounge finishing some last minute proofreading work for the ELJ. I didn't usually sit in the lounge, but Betty wanted the article by noon and the lounge was the most efficient place to work. If Betty were looking for me, she would have no trouble finding me.

Terrence Washington sat down across from me and began to work the daily crossword puzzle. "Work due yesterday?" he asked.

"You got it."

I kept reading, flipping pages. People came and sat around me. The woman on my left explained to someone passing through that she had worn the same jacket the night before. The guy next to her hadn't read a case for class. He knew the facts and the holding, though; he could fake the rest.

"Ike's partner?" Washington said.

"Mamie," I said.

"Four letters."

"Tina," said the guy who hadn't read the assigned case.

Around ten o'clock, most of the students in the lounge headed off to class, leaving me working and Washington with his crossword.

"I had some moles taken off," Washington said.

"What?" I didn't understand.

"I've had five moles taken off in the past two years.... Does that bother you?"

"No, go on."

"The last one was on my back. The doctor found some bad stuff in it. I have to stay out of the sun."

"You just have to wear a hat. You can do that."

"Yeah."

Washington went back to his crossword. He wanted to know the name of a river in Spain. I couldn't help him.

Betty saw me hurriedly finishing the Conroy article. I finished and gave her my changes. It wasn't bad. I had improved on Francis' version a little, making a few minor changes.

"No queries?" she asked. "No tabs?"

"It was pretty good," I said. "Besides, it was written by a senator. I didn't feel comfortable making wholesale changes, especially at this stage. I thought changes at this stage got pretty expensive."

"Listen, even at this stage, if we need to make changes, we'll make the changes. I know Trisha said we need to keep costs down, but since then we've ... found more money. I just want to make sure this thing is right."

"This is pretty good," I said, leaving the article with her and heading off to B.E.

(2:15 p.m.)

Monday hadn't been a good day to miss B.E. I knew it wouldn't be. Tarenzella went over financial accounting, balance sheets, income statements. There were formulas for figuring operating profit and net profit, working capital, current ratio, liquidity ratio, book value, inventory, various approaches to valuing a company, and more. It was a lot of material from a book I no longer had time to read. If I had gone to class, at least I could have learned what Tarenzella thought was important.

After class, I caught Francis in the hallway and asked if I had missed anything important. He offered me his notes.

"That would be great," I said. "I just need to see what she went over."

"I didn't take very good notes."

"It would still be a help."

I was a little desperate. I had to have those notes.

(2:50 p.m.)

Dear Mr. Westphal:

On behalf of the firm, I want to thank you for your letter of October 25 to T. Randall Parker, Esq. inquiring about summer employment with Witmer, Neel & DeSilvas. Your interest in the firm is sincerely appreciated and we thank you for writing.

We are fortunate to receive a great number of resumes each year from qualified candidates and thus have many difficult employment decisions to make. Although you have excellent qualifications, we regret we are unable to invite you to interview with us at this time. Because circumstances change from year to year, however, this letter should not be construed in any way

that would discourage you from contacting us during
your third year.

Thank you again for your interest. We wish you every
success during the remainder of the school year.

Sincerely yours,

Ronald S. Gould
Chairman, Recruiting Committee

RSG:mfs

(3:45 p.m.)

I sat down and wrote thank you notes to everyone I had met at
Gaines, eleven letters, each touching on something discussed during the
interview or over dinner, each trying to make that final impression that
would put me ahead of the next guy or gal. It was another couple of
hours I could have better spent. With each letter, I had to put on
another smile, wrack my brain for something clever and interesting and
appropriate to say. I might have been more enthusiastic if I thought the
letters would make a difference in whether I got a job, but I wasn't sure.
The evaluations on me were due immediately after each interview. I had
caught a glimpse of the form the attorneys filled out on an associate's
desk. Still, I had to make the effort. There was the possibility that some
of these people were members of the Recruiting Committee and would
have a chance to say something nice about me later. And of course if I
did get the job, these letters would be another step toward establishing
rapport with the people at the firm.

Some of the letters were easy. During my interview with James Cole,
I told him about the pizza place in Bexley where Bob Greene had hung
out in high school, but I couldn't recall its name. When I got home, I
called the Bexley Public Library and got the name right off. I passed it
along. Sheila White, I had learned, had an apartment near my parents.
Because she was new to Columbus, I thought I would recommend a

good place to eat in the area, Panzera's Pizza. It was frequently named one of the best pizza places in the city. I knew the family. They attended my church. And they made great pizza.

Other letters were difficult. I wanted to do a little more than just thank the person for the interview and say I looked forward to seeing them again. In Mr. Duncan's letter, I had to find a way to refer to my work on the Environmental Law Journal. Kimball's letter was also difficult. I let Katie read the first draft, which tried to explain the predicament she had put me in. Katie frowned, so I ripped it up and wrote Kimball a gracious letter thanking her for a very enjoyable trip. My letter to Allen Dowd, one of the fellows I'd had lunch with, was also difficult. I finally wrote that I was interested to learn that one of his favorite authors was Kurt Vonnegut. While I hadn't read *Slaughterhouse Five* in a number of years, our discussion had me looking forward to reading it again—as well as seeing the movie. "As I recall," I wrote, "Valerie Perrine is outstanding." This last bit was written for the bachelor in him. Valerie Perrine wasn't shy about revealing her better attributes.

To make sure all of the letters arrived, I put all of the envelopes in one package and mailed it to Kimball. She could forward them to the various parties through inter-office mail. I put the package in the corner mailbox, thinking, with some amusement, that Kimball could only wonder what I had written when I stopped in my tracks, seized with sudden panic. All of my letters had been so carefully prepared, striking just the right tone. If they were all routed back to Kimball for my file, for the Recruiting Committee, they would all shine in their own way. *Kenneth? Nice young fellow.* No one could say different. *But what was this about Valerie Perrine?* How could I have been so stupid! Valerie Perrine! The name was synonymous with full figure. What kind of person would write such a thing in professional correspondence? It was at best a juvenile reference, at worst highly sexist ...

But I was already trying to argue my way out. Wasn't what I had written the equivalent of writing, say, Peter O'Toole was excellent? Almost nearly but not quite hardly. Discussion of sexism in the workplace was at an apex. Small mistakes about big matters could have a way of creating havoc. Last summer, one of the clerks I had worked with at Simoneaux sealed his fate when a package of brownies arrived for him at the firm. Every picture tells a story.

I couldn't fool myself. The letter would kill me. The letter would make me a laughing stock unless—I had a thought—unless the letter was too embarrassing for Allen to pass along. Of course. There was no way he could pass the letter along without reflecting somehow on himself, his own views, the image of himself projected to the world and reflected in me. He would see the letter before anyone else. Kimball wasn't going to open his mail. He was smart. He would see the ramifications. And once he saw, he would make sure the letter never found its way back into circulation. He might have enjoyed this little laugh at my expense, he might have been tempted to send it on, but in the final analysis he just couldn't do it. That was what I finally decided. That thought made me feel better. Regardless of what he thought of me, in self-preservation, as much as it might have pained him, he would have to cover up Valerie Perrine.

November 14
(Thursday)
(2:30 p.m.)

Muder began class by saying that if we understood what happened Tuesday, we understood the hardest part of the course.

Great.

I tried to read the notes of the woman sitting next to me. "Do you want to copy them?" she asked.

"No ... well, let me see here."

Muder was talking about an Air Quality Control Region (AQCR) in Utah. Each of its two stacks emitted 100 tons of a pollutant. The proposal was to scrap one stack and add another that would emit 150 tons. The effect was a fallout "footprint" drifting toward a second AQCR. *What the heck was she talking about?* In AQCR I, the SO2 footprint went up by 10, the CO footprint by 20. In AQCR II, the SO2 footprint went up by 5, the CO footprint by 10. Both regions were attainment for SO2. Region I was attainment for CO and Region II was nonattainment.

"Can the refinery do it?" Muder asked.

Do what?

"What requirements will the refinery have to make? What limitations for such emissions? Go through the nonattainment drill, the PSD drill, and the transport drill."

I was trying to listen while reading Angie's notes. I tried to whisper a few questions, but Angie was in the crash position as well. Muder was flying at a high altitude, and many of us were having trouble drawing a breath. I concentrated on everything she said so I would have a chance to make sense of it later. The method had worked well enough the year before. Just don't panic. The most complicated things somehow make sense upon reflection. Sometimes ...

Under the AQCR drill, there are 4 results based on the variance provisions, 4 ways to wiggle out. Despite the coverage, if you twist the federal land manager's arm, he might let it fly. Is there a standard for his certification? Does he have a duty under subsection (ii)? If you can prove he got a call from the president, it would be dereliction of duty. Variances? If the facility affects a Class I area, that can be a varianced AQCR under certain circumstances. Skip the (d) drill. PSD increments measure how much pollution one can add from the baseline. Today, in the West, there are additional severity of tight increments but additional variance of (c) drill. The transport problem provides 4 possibilities for any pollutant crossing AQCRs: PSD to NA; PSD to PSD; NA to NA; and NA to PSD. In PSD to PSD, if there is no baseline, you get a free lunch up to the NAAQS; if the baseline is set, you can only consume up to the increment and then you have to offset. PSD to NA, you have to use NAAQS. NA to NA or to

PSD, see (C) offsets. If offset by better than one to one, abatement at the source ...

Some of it made sense later, some didn't.

When I got around to looking at the notes Jonathan had dropped off, they didn't help much, either. He liked to draw pictures of factories in his notes.

Smoke poured from the stacks.

12

November 14
(Thursday)

Following my interview with Gaines, my assessment of my chances for
an offer continued to fluctuate. On the one hand, they had paid several
hundred dollars to fly me out, another hundred to feed me, and attorneys had taken time out of their day to meet with me, which amounted
to another several hundred dollars in billable hours. They had a good-
sized investment in me. Still, there would inevitably be heavy politics
involved in the selection. I was surely competing with others as good or
better qualified. Who knew, really, what would happen? Each day that
passed without word brought more uncertainty. The longer they took
to make the decision, the more it looked like they wanted to give me a
job, that they were trying to give me a job, that the decision was
extremely difficult ... and the easier it would be for them to make pro-
fuse apologies and send me on my way.

Eventually, I quit jumping every time the phone rang and began to
look more closely at the letters that seemed to hold some promise. One
was from Fielding & Watt, the Cleveland law firm with whom I had
been trying to get an interview for months, most recently by dropping
the name of Fay Rubenstein, a woman who worked with my uncle.
Their reply offered me an interview if I was in Ohio at Thanksgiving:

Dear Mr. Westphal:

Harry Canton has forwarded your October 25th letter with your resume to our Recruiting Committee for review. Thank you for writing Harry, as your letter reminded those of us on the Recruiting Committee that we had not yet followed up on our exchange of letters at the end of the summer. I apologize for our delay in getting back to you.

We would enjoy meeting with you when you return to Ohio for Christmas break. I would ask that you call Claudette Villiere, our Recruiting Coordinator, to arrange a specific date for you to drop by. Our interview process normally includes a morning of interviews and then lunch with several associates. If by chance you are planning to be in Ohio around Thanksgiving, we could instead schedule an interview at that time. Our recruiting process for summer associate positions normally wraps up by early to mid December, so if you are going to be [in] Ohio over Thanksgiving, that time frame might work better for all concerned.

Once again, you have my sincere apologies for our tardiness in getting back in touch with you. We look forward to meeting you.

> Best regards,
>
> Jerome P. Thorson

JPT/leb
cc: Harold T. Canton, Esq.
Ms. Claudette Villiere

They would obviously need a certain amount of lead time to set up the interviews, so I would have to let them know within the week. I almost couldn't believe it when I looked at my calendar: Thanksgiving was only two weeks away.

November 15
(Friday)

Pretty regularly, perhaps twice a month, Career Services put a listing of jobs in our folders at school. The jobs were broken down by state, gathered from career services offices across the country, perhaps from alumni or government offices as well. I read them straight through, always with the sense that these far off jobs would be snatched up long before my letters were even typed. The judge's neighbor's daughter would have the job. As with the stock market, the big money was always way out in front. Still, twice a month, I scanned the announcements for jobs and just as quickly added the paper to the recycling bin.

Today, though, Career Services had left a letter sealed in an envelope: I had been granted an interview with Willey, Craig & Greene, in Metairie, Louisiana. I scarcely remembered applying with Willey, Craig, so many times did I walk over to the Career Services Office and put resumes with attached cover letters in the boxes lining the shelves. That afternoon I called Dee Dee and set up an interview for Wednesday, November 27, at 5:00 p.m.

Perhaps this would be the one. Metairie had some nice neighborhoods. The fact sheet Career Services attached to the letter told me something about the firm. Willey, Craig & Greene was a litigation firm, with insurance and corporate clients. With 11 partners, 12 associates, and a support staff of 83, the firm, the materials said, "has made a specialty of providing the most cost efficient service to its many clients." I'll bet, I thought, imagining for a minute the result if all law firms relied so heavily on support staff.

Well, I'd give it a shot.

In the meantime, letters continued to fill my mailbox at home. The rejection finally arrived from Witteman, Waits. They evidently could get along without my friend's little business. The letter was from the girl, a stick with rouge. That was my only image. I didn't think I could have recognized her on the street.

Other letters I tacked on the bulletin board above my desk, letters offering hope, fingers beckoning me forward, keep walking, just a little farther. If I would travel to Cleveland, if I could wait until Christmas, if I could drink water standing on my head, someone somewhere looked forward to seeing me. They all wanted to *see* me. They would have me traveling all over the country just to count the moles on my face. People are accepted into almost all law schools with no interview whatsoever. Tulane discourages them. Law schools often discourage them. What people look like has nothing to do with whether they will succeed in law school, whether they can learn the elements of a contract and talk about how the rule might apply to a given set of facts. But if you want a job, they all wanted to *see* you. They want to see whether you can make small talk, whether you can use a fork, whether you have an easy laugh, whether you'll be wearing a toupee some day and whether it will likely be rough around the edges. These things are not prerequisites to going to law school, any law school, but if you want a job, they all looked forward to *seeing* you.

Well, perhaps all of them would get to see me, perhaps none of them would. It all depended on Gaines. If Gaines fell through and I had to fly back to Ohio, I would try to meet as many people in as short a period as I could. If worst came to worst, I could work as a volunteer at the Environmental Protection Agency. A recent letter from the Agency seemed to shut the door on a clerkship, but opened up the possibility of volunteer work, another way to put my summer to good use:

> Dear Mr. Westphal:
> On behalf of Daniel Tynan, Acting Assistant Administrator, thank you for your letter expressing interest in the summer law clerk program with the

Office of Enforcement. Although you have excellent qualifications, I must regrettably inform you that we have selected other candidates for the summer law clerk program. However, in the event that you are interested in pursuing a volunteer position either during the summer or during the school year, please contact Ms. Joslyn Fink for further information.

Best wishes in your future legal studies and your professional career.

Sincerely,

Peter E. English
Hiring Committee Coordinator

I had some options. Something would happen. Meanwhile, I had other things to worry about ...

November 17
(Sunday)

Saturday afternoon I got a call from Madeline Matthews saying she wanted to get together to talk about boosting subscriptions for the ELJ. I had mentioned an interest in doing just that on my application for assistant editor, hadn't I?

"Of course," I said.

We met in the student lounge Sunday night. It helped that I didn't know how to use a computer to address letters and envelopes.

"I'll have to find someone with a computer," she said.

"Yeah." I was careful not to say too much. Sure, I had written passionately about boosting subscriptions, but they had waited far too long to expect too much. I really didn't have the time to spare anymore.

We sat down, and I proofread a letter she planned to send to libraries across the country. I suggested she raise the subscription price and offer a discount of five or ten dollars if people replied by the end of January. I really didn't have much more to say.

I left her in the lounge looking over her letter and went upstairs to copy a few of Landrow's past exams. He had a reputation for giving multiple-choice exams with answers that differed by only a word or two, forcing choices between gray and grayish. I had heard, though, that some of his questions were taken straight from old exams. I would make copies and try to read them later.

*   *   *

We were now beginning the 13th week of the semester. With exams a few weeks away, it was time to come up with a plan if I was to get through standing. For Remedies, I purchased Smith's Review, which Worth had recommended earlier in the semester, saying that if we were going to read one of the prepared outlines, we might as well read a good one. He had read them all, he said, and Smith's was the best. He even asked the bookstore to order enough for the class. For B.E., I was re-reading the casebook, making an outline as I went along, marching through fiduciary issues, property rights of partners, and dissolution of the partnership. In Pollution Control, I was counting on my class notes with a vague plan to re-read the important cases.

I was probably making the most progress in Evidence. Both B.E. and Evidence were closed book exams, which meant that I'd need to have an outline in my head going in or risk drawing a blank. Over the weekend, I had finished going through my class notes, reviewing all of the problems we had gone over in class. I had purchased an Emanuel's Outline, a Nutshell, and a set of flashcards. Katie got a computer program from Loyola. I hoped that repetition would sharpen my skills. Although I had yet to get through much of this material, I had read the summary outline in Emanuel's and found it excellent. That, I decided, would be my outline, the focus of my study. In Evidence, there were rules upon rules and exceptions to exceptions, but they were all laid out. I just had to find time to read them and think about them and read them again.

November 18
(Monday)

A lawyer, an engineer, and the pope died and went to Heaven. St. Peter met them at the Pearly Gates, loaded them in his car, and started driving. He drove into a middle-class neighborhood, with tree-lined streets and well-kept yards, stopped before a house, and told the engineer, "Here is where you will spend eternity." The engineer hopped off, and St. Peter drove on. The neighborhoods got nicer and nicer. St. Peter stopped before a most beautiful mansion, with palm trees and pool, tennis courts and fountains and sculpted gardens and acres of manicured lawn, and he told the lawyer, "Here is where you will spend eternity." The lawyer hopped off, and St. Peter drove on. Now the pope was starting to get excited. But as St. Peter drove on, they emerged once again in a middle-class neighborhood and stopped before a plain two-story house. "Here is where you will spend eternity," St. Peter said to the pope.

The pope looked around and said, "I don't mean any disrespect, but there must be some mistake. You see, on Earth, I was the pope, and you gave the lawyer a beautiful mansion."

"No mistake," St. Peter said, "There are lots of popes up here, but he's the only lawyer."

That Landrow had continued to tell jokes throughout the semester was at first surprising, but lately I had begun to see his jokes as an appropriate part of our education, a means of deadening our senses to the often open animosity held by much of the population toward lawyers. We were learning to laugh at the worst manifestations of our professional personas: the arrogant lawyer, the greedy lawyer, the wicked lawyer.... We were learning to displace ourselves. That was someone else. That was just a joke ...

The recent topic in Evidence class had been dying declarations. A victim's dying declaration, under the common law, is admissible as evidence if the declarant is dead at the time of trial (the death need not be caused by the defendant), the declarant is aware of his impending death, and the declaration relates to the homicidal act or circumstances. The theory was that a person who believes he's about to die will tell the truth.

"It has something to do with wanting to make things right with one's maker," Landrow explained, "which is pure nonsense. That's one of the good things about my book—"

"You mean the ninety-dollar book?" hollered Claire Brunetti from the side of the room.

"I think it's ninety-five dollars," Landrow said. "You'd know that if you had bought it."

"I have it right here," Claire said. "It's too valuable to leave at home. I'm afraid I might get robbed."

Landrow smiled. A rare defeat.

With three weeks left in the semester, Landrow had covered only about half of the material on the course outline. So when he announced that he planned to get through all of the material by the end of the semester, even some of the students who were conscientiously slogging through the textbook began to think about cutting corners. Jonathan began to take a survey of people who were reading the book. I was not inclined to tell Jonathan my thoughts on the matter. I had not read the textbook for weeks and had no inclination to start, but that was nothing to brag about. Jonathan waited for an answer, looking ready to chuck the reading if he could only assure himself that others were also ready to abandon ship.

November 19
(Tuesday)

He had misplaced the first one I left in his mailbox asking if he might say something nice should someone inquire, so I printed up another and hoped for better luck this time.

"I'm sorry I misplaced your letter," he told me as we walked down the hall toward his office.

"I thought maybe you just wanted to see how dedicated I was," I said. "It also crossed my mind that you threw it out and thought better of it." I was playing paranoid games with him. I thought it might bring us closer together.

We sat down in his office and stared at one another.

"I see you worked at Simoneaux last summer," he said. "How did you enjoy that?"

"I'm not sure I know what you mean."

"Many people don't like working at large firms."

"It was all right," I said. "It was fun. Lots of lunches. You know ..."

He nodded, trying to decide whether I was just being evasive or whether I was a complete idiot. In truth, the summer had been a blur. I couldn't recall the details of any of the projects on which I had worked. Even general topics would be difficult to come up with on the spot. What I remembered were the big lunches: Monday Cuban platters, Wednesday Chinese all you can eat buffets, Thursday Mother's red beans and rice. Sometimes I would be so full after lunch it was all I could do to get back to the office and keep my head off my desk. One of the associates kept caffeine pills in his desk, and the clerks were invited to make use of them freely.

"The clerks see the best part of a law firm, I suppose," I added.

He had to agree. Lawyers work hard and play hard. After the work, any work, any sustained self-denial, some reward is in order. It is easy to justify the food, the drinks, the cocktail parties, the bonuses, vacations, expense accounts, stocks, mini-malls, land deals, drinks, homes, cars, paintings, clothing, sunroofs, tennis courts, sailboats, horses, junkets, shoes, sunshine, swimming pools....They splurge. They spend. After all, they earned it. And the clerks go along like hostages on a shooting spree, taking in every word their captors say.

November 20
(Wednesday)

No article to edit, no casenote to write, no interview to prepare for, dress for, go to. I found, to my surprise, I had a morning to myself and almost didn't know what to do. I went to the library and read B.E. We were responsible for the chapter on securities—common stock, preferred stock, equity, warrants and options, debt securities, and the like. The casebook said that common stock, preferred stock, and debt could be viewed as if on a spectrum of risk and reward. I liked spectrums. I liked any attempt to visualize the law, but I couldn't quite grasp what distinguished common stock from preferred stock from debt. It couldn't be a difficult concept. The book was throwing out distinguishing factors. I was making lists. It all seemed hopelessly overlapped and confusing. The owners of common stock could elect directors, might receive dividends, and possessed an interest in the assets. The owners of preferred stock had a preference for dividends, liquidation preference, and various options, such as a right to convert.

I tried to skim the material once quickly, to give myself an overview, a frame of reference. It was one of those pieces of advice you hear in high school that finally makes sense when you study the law: skim the material, read the headings, get a sense of where the material is going before you get started. If the casebook had just come out and said that the labels were meaningless, I would have been a lot better off. Of course, when you are behind in class, it is difficult to sit down and read the material with the requisite attention. You aren't smart enough. You can't keep up. You've beaten time all of you're life, but now you can't understand why your legs don't move as fast as you thought they did, why you can't get by on five hours of sleep, why you end up reading a single sentence again and again and again. You long for a nap, feel a cold coming on, linger in front of the television … and you start to believe every bad word uttered in your general direction.

Dear Mr. Westphal:

Thank you for your recent letter requesting to be interviewed during your Christmas break.

As you might expect, given today's job market, we are being careful in the number of offers which we have outstanding at any one time. As of this date, we have interviewed many students who we have seen on-campus, extended several offers and received several acceptances. It is for this reason that we cannot invite you to interview with Arter & Hadden at this time or during your Christmas break. However, we remain genuinely interested in you and will be back in touch with you if we have room in our class after we hear from all of our outstanding offers.

Thank you for your interest in Arter & Hadden and taking the time to contact us.

Very truly yours,
ARTER & HADDEN

Rose Campbell,
Director of Legal Recruiting

*   *   *

Dear Mr. Westphal:

We have received your letter and resume and appreciate your interest in Thompson, Hine and Flory.

As you probably know, we interview hundreds of students on law school campuses and receive a large number of additional inquiries as well. From among the many qualified applicants, we have invited a limited number of students to visit our offices for further discussions. Our requirements for summer associates will be filled from among these students, and I, therefore, regret to inform you that we will not be pursuing your application.

We wish you every success in your efforts to locate a position for next summer.

Very truly yours,

Martha H. Bardach, Esq.
Recruiting Coordinator

MHB/amq

*   *   *

Dear Mr. Westphal:

As a member of our firm's professional Hiring Committee, I received your resume and request to be considered for summer employment at Baker & Hostetler.

Despite your fine credentials, we cannot extend to you an invitation for an interview at our office. The competition for positions is particularly intense, as we have many qualified applicants and a limited number of positions available. I can only assure you that your application was carefully considered.

Your interest in Baker & Hostetler is sincerely appreciated. We wish you success next summer and in your future endeavors.

Very truly yours,

Aston D. Aikman

ADA:07700:00150:2L:BTR-72.COD
sesd 11/17/00

*   *   *

Dear Mr. Westphal:

Thank you for your recent expression of interest in our summer program.

I am sorry to report that we are not currently in a position to take advantage of your availability. It is my judgment that we have already extended a sufficient number of offers to second-year law students to fill the positions available next summer.

If that situation changes, I shall certainly contact you promptly. Your resume is impressive and you may be assured that we shall keep you in mind.

Very truly yours,

Adam G. Blackman

AGB/jel

13

Landrow was marching us through a discussion on expert witnesses, giving us his usual variety of tips. At trial, lay the foundation by bringing up the witness's education, experience, special training, teaching, publications, and, most important, "the big number":

—Doctor, how many times have you performed a similar operation?

—I'd say about ten thousand times.

When you are deposing the other side's expert, get her to talk and talk. These people are busy, they are rarely completely prepared, but no expert will ever say, "I don't know." Appear stupid and keep them talking. And of course you can always try to impeach on the ground of bias:

—You are being paid for your testimony here today, doctor, isn't that correct?

—Yes, I am.

—And it's a good fee, isn't that correct?

—It's adequate.

—You are being paid two hundred dollars an hour, isn't that correct?

—Yes.

—That's more than adequate, isn't it, doctor?

*   *   *

That afternoon, I found, to my horror, a letter from Gaines in my mailbox at home. Not a good sign. They surely would have called if I were being offered a job. Now I just had a thin impersonal letter. There would be another trip to Ohio, more interviews, more money spent, more time away from school. I opened the letter with my books still in my hand:

> Dear Ken:
> Thank you for your kind note. I will be going to Rubino's as soon as possible to check out the pizza and the Bob Greene picture.
> I enjoyed talking with you while you were in town, and wish you the best.
> Sincerely,
>
> James W. Cole
> JWC:rsd

I read the letter a couple of times, wondering if I had missed something, if he was writing on behalf of the firm, if the firm was expressing its regrets, if he was trying to tell me something. He wished me the best. What did that mean? Was I out? Was I supposed to accept other offers that came along? He was one of the movers and shakers at the firm. His word would carry weight. Was this the kindest rejection letter of all time?

I put the letter back in the envelope and left it on the stereo speaker in the living room so Katie would see it when she came home. She could enjoy the same moment of excitement and concern I had when I saw the return address. A moment of excitement was something. A little fantasy. It only costs a dollar to play the lottery. For pocket change you can dream of a new truck, paying your bills, buying a house or a new set of false teeth, and making everyone you ever knew suck air. Applying to law schools is a lot like the lottery. You send stuff out. You assess your chances. You wait. When you are accepted, you feel like a millionaire. Only later do you realize that in this lottery you are the one who pays ...

"Did you see the letter?" I asked Katie later.

She had. She seemed a little down, something I hadn't foreseen. I expect the worst. She expects the best. I felt bad.

... Of course, there are students every year who realize their dream of being accepted to law school and drop out a few days or weeks into the program.

Dreamers.

... And some come back for one reason or another, as if they had no other choice. Louis Auchincloss left the practice of law to write, only to return. His autobiography never really explains this turnabout. Of course, such omissions are the submerged part of the iceberg that moves one's life along, a wise man wandering out into the cold in search of a tropical island or a kid crying for his lost father.

"What do you think?" I asked. "Was it a rejection letter?"

"It's not a rejection letter."

"It's just a nice response to the letter I'd sent him. He's a nice guy. Still, I have to wonder if he's trying to tell me something."

"It's just a thank you note."

I tried to believe that, too.

*   *   *

Thanksgiving was now less than a week away. I could no longer put off making arrangements for a second trip to Ohio. Besides, I had now received an invitation to visit Branegan, Reed, Dowd & Spatz "if my travels took me to Columbus." It looked as if they would. That made two interviews I could arrange while I was home: Branegan, Reed in Columbus and Fielding & Watt in Cleveland.

I called Claudette Villiere, the recruiting coordinator at Fielding & Watt. If Gaines was going to pass on me, Fielding was my next best shot.

My uncle sent them business. They had a strong environmental practice. And it was their delay in getting back to me that was forcing me to make a second trip now, over Thanksgiving, a week from finals. Claudette seemed happy to hear from me. I told her I could meet on Friday, November 29th, the day after Thanksgiving.

"One of our few holidays," she said. "Would Monday be okay?"

Monday was terrible. It was the last week of classes. I would have to miss B.E. again. Although Tarenzella had promised us early in the semester to avoid the "Force five-hundred," a reference to Professor Force's famous march through 500 pages during the last two weeks of class several years before, she was moving at breakneck pace in an effort to stick to her syllabus, lecturing almost exclusively, trying to give us a sense of what was most important. Monday was also the last class of Evidence. Not only would Landrow hit the highlights of two assigned chapters, he would be discussing the exam.

Monday was terrible.

"Monday will be fine," I told her.

That was that. I would be going to Ohio over Thanksgiving. I called Branegan, Reed to squeeze in another interview, if possible, late Monday afternoon. The recruiting coordinator seemed downright discouraging, but I pressed ahead and scheduled to meet her at four-thirty Monday afternoon.

Then I called Mr. Payne, who, based on the fact that his wife worked with my mother, had suggested the possibility of an interview with his firm when I was in Columbus. He wasn't in. I left a message that Kenneth Westphal had called. What a strange message he would have when he returned. But he would figure out what it was all about, and he would figure out why I never called back.

My sister-in-law worked for AAA, so I called her about airplane tickets. I would leave Sunday evening, arrive in Columbus at one in the morning, get a few hours of sleep, and head for Cleveland before daybreak. The interviews would begin at nine o'clock. I would speak with seven lawyers, have lunch with three, and be back in Columbus in time for my four-thirty interview with Branegan, Reed. After the interview, I would have a quick dinner with my parents and make it back to the airport for my seven o'clock flight back to New Orleans.

The cost for the trip: $740.00. I charged the tickets to my credit card.

November 26
(Tuesday)

While the CWA and the CAA both sought to deal with pollution by focusing on the end of the pipe, other laws had attempted to deal with the front end, to put restrictions on things that produced "unreasonable adverse effects." We were studying TSCA and California Proposition 65. All Muder wanted us to see were the various standards for approving the use of different substances.

We began with TSCA, a 1970s statute bent on placing safety first in the regulation of pesticides. After all, it was the misuse of the pesticide DDT that had kicked off the environmental movement. The goal of TSCA was to evaluate substances before placing them in commerce. Identify what is coming in. Determine if testing is required. Determine if there is an unreasonable risk. Suspend or cancel the chemical.

But TSCA had only regulated six substances in 20 years.

Why hadn't the program worked?

"It takes an average of four years to sort through the literature and make an assessment," Muder said. "It costs $4.4 million per chemical just to get the numbers. If the assessment shows carcinogenicity, a cost/benefit analysis is conducted." What is an "unreasonable risk" is, after all, a judgment call. Of some 62,000 chemicals, perhaps 30 have been tested thoroughly.

Why hadn't the program worked?

"Congress passed the ball," Muder said, answering her own question. "There are some places where regulators don't dare to tread: the free road, the green lawn, the sanctity of the bathroom."

At what point do we act?

How many must die?

What's an unreasonable risk?

California declared war on chemicals with Proposition 65. Drafted by the Environmental Defense Fund and passed by popular vote over industry objection, the proposition does basically two things. First, it creates a duty to warn. Warnings must be on all labels. Second, the statute gives industry a duty to refrain from discharging the worst of the worst, carcinogens and reproductive toxins that are sold to consumers or put in a source of drinking water.

"This is a statute with some bite," Muder said, leading us through the inevitable loopholes.

*   *   *

Remedies class that afternoon was canceled, although I didn't realize it right away. I walked on into the classroom, planning to put a note on the lectern before Worth arrived. I didn't think I could take his "I'm in on the joke" expression. Another note was already there:

> **Prof Worth —**
> **I will not be able to participate today. My parents are**
> **in town visiting.**
>
> **Judy Oliver**

Worth hated explanations. He told us the first day of class he didn't want to hear any explanations. *Prof Worth, I had to rush my roommate to the hospital last night with food poisoning. She'll never eat blowfish again! Prof Worth, I read the wrong assignment.... I got lucky.... My menstrual cramps are killing me ...*

But there was nobody in the classroom. It was eleven o'clock. Did I have the wrong day? I had done that before, confused the days. No. This was Tuesday. Had everyone disappeared? Was I the only sinner on Earth?

I went out in the hall and found the yellow notice next to the door saying that class had been canceled. Make-up, the notice said, would be Monday at five o'clock. Another class I would miss because of the trip to Columbus. That made three. I was least concerned with Remedies. People missed Remedies all the time. Besides, this was a make-up class at an awkward time on a day we didn't ordinarily meet.

I stayed just long enough to tape Judy's note to the blackboard. The world needs love, but if you haven't got love you might as well have laughter.

November 27
(Wednesday)

The day before Thanksgiving break I was working through the Remedies casebook, reviewing class notes and highlighting the important material that followed each case, hoping to go through it all again later, a quick review closer to the exam.

I was making my way through declaratory judgments when Jonathan stopped by the apartment, suggesting we tour the cemetery down the street. He had his camera around his neck. I looked out the window. It was a beautiful day. The cemetery was a fun place to visit, historic, eerie. The walls surrounding the block were thick with remains of smallpox victims, the family mausoleums elaborate. A few weeks before, Katie and I had watched a country rock band recreate a jazz funeral procession for a music video. I invited Jonathan to take a seat and put my feet up on the card table spread with the Remedies notes I planned to review over the next few days.

"I can't, really," I said, "I have an interview."

"OOOOh."

"I don't want to go. They never lead anywhere."

"I've had sixteen. The rejection letters are pasted on my refrigerator."

"That's a confidence builder each morning."

I walked outside with him. I was going to drive through a fast food place for lunch. I deserved a break. At the doorstep, I stopped to check my mail. There was the rejection letter from Hanssen, Hess, the firm where I had spent an entire afternoon sitting in the boardroom and succeeded only in embarrassing the interviewer. I opened it and started to read:

> Dear Mr. Westphal:
>
> I enjoyed our interview on October 30. After reviewing our projected needs with other members of our Recruiting Committee, it appears that we will not have an opening available for you. We shall keep your resume in our files in the event that something should change in this regard.
>
> Again, thank you for interviewing with us and with every good wish for your future success, I am
>
> Sincerely,
>
> David Donnelly
>
> :dd
> 07050000\692.JAA\REJECT.9

REJECT. There it was at the bottom of the letter. A nicely written letter, I supposed, but all I could see was the word, in small print, sure, but there, on the page, in capital letters no less: REJECT. Not even any pretense of concern. Why did he even wait three weeks to send it out? Why wasn't it just waiting for me when I got home? Firms have letters for all occasions and situations, like briefs or contracts, all ready to go. They just sit on them. That way you think they go through all kinds of agony, you think they are doing all kinds of work on your behalf, then BAM!

you get a bill for eight hundred dollars or a letter offering every good wish for your future success.

"I never read those letters," Jonathan said, trying to see who the letter was from. "I just scan them for the key words."

"I don't read them, either, really, I suppose."

"I had figured, at last resort, I could hook up with a public interest job," Jonathan said. "Now even that looks bad."

"Yeah. Did you turn in your secured transactions paper this morning? I saw you out the window. It looked like you were on your way to turn it in."

"I only went down to the grocery store."

He led me to his car and took his secured transactions paper from the back seat.

"It's heavy," I said, turning a few pages. "It's a real advantage having only four exams." I was still trying to explain why I couldn't tour the cemetery.

Jonathan didn't say anything. Of course, since dropping Federal Procedure, I was taking only four classes myself. I hadn't told anyone, but we talked enough about our classes that he may have suspected as much. He put on his sunglasses and headed off to finish his roll of film.

After lunch, I called the EPA in Washington, D.C., wanting to learn more about volunteer positions. "The thought of working for the EPA appeals to me intuitively," I told Joslyn Fink, the woman in charge of the program.

We had only just begun our conversation when my phone began to beep. Someone was trying to reach me. I would have normally ignored the call, but I thought there was a good chance it might be Gaines, trying to reach me before Thanksgiving break.

"I'm sorry," I said. "This may be important."

Joslyn was willing to wait.

It was Dee Dee, the secretary from Willey, Craig & Greene, the Metairie firm fueled by paralegals. She wanted to know if I could reschedule my interview for the following Wednesday, same time. She had forgotten when we had scheduled the appointment that it was the day before Thanksgiving. I agreed, of course. I couldn't keep my interviewers from their Thanksgiving vacation.

"Thank you," I told Joslyn, "that was important. Could you tell me what I might expect as a volunteer at the EPA?"

"Of course it would be better if you were on a work/study program through school," she said, "then we could assign you to an attorney who'd oversee your work. If you're not working for school credit, you'll take projects like all the other clerks."

I wanted to be very sure about this point. Tulane had no work/study program, and as a volunteer, I feared I might end up taking orders from some sadsack who jumped at the chance to have a law student at his disposal, who was already beginning to have some vague idea that now the data base he had dreamed of for years might finally get off the ground ... and I would end up organizing the pile of junk he had let accumulate on his desk and typing the names of defunct magazines into his personal computer, which, he imagined, would make him indispensable to the general counsel and might even get him out of that basement office.

"You'll be treated like all the other clerks," she promised.

*   *   *

I must have received fifty rejection letters in October and November. After all of the compliments, the hollow promises, the tortured language, one letter seemed to stand out from the rest. It was from the Cleveland office of Jones, Day, Reavis & Pogue, one of the largest law firms in the world, with offices in Atlanta, Austin, Brussels, Chicago, Columbus, Cleveland, Dallas, Frankfurt, Geneva, Hong Kong, Irvine, London, Los Angeles, New York, Paris, Pittsburgh, Riyadh, Taipei, Tokyo, and Washington, D.C.:

997545-206-060

Dear Mr. Westphal:

Thank you for your inquiry expressing an interest in a summer associate position with the Cleveland Office of Jones Day. We appreciate your interest in the Firm and our practice.

Unfortunately, our current hiring needs do not permit us to consider you for a summer position.

Thank you again for your interest in Jones Day and best wishes during the remaining school year.

Very truly yours,

Matthew G. Rafferty

That was a smooth letter, I thought. Thank you for your interest. Unfortunately, we can't hire you. Thank you for your interest. No bull about keeping the letter on file. No windy explanations. No hollow compliments. This was a form letter that wasn't trying to be anything other than a form letter.

I appreciated that.

14

I told Katie I would go to Cleveland if she promised to attend two classes for me, Evidence and Business. She was noncommittal. I was especially interested in what Tarenzella would say. At least Katie had to go to B.E. After some negotiating with Katie and an attempt to reach Tarenzella by telephone, I finally told Katie, "Just show up before class and give the tape recorder to Tommy Wong." Then it occurred to me that Tommy was in both Evidence and B.E. and would be able to record both classes. Simple.

Still, I was a little uncertain about asking him. The tension of the Compadre Club interview continued to stilt our attempts at conversation. He would hardly be sympathetic that I was leaving town for another job interview. And he hadn't asked me for notes since early in the semester, notes for which he had long since reciprocated. That was probably why the idea hadn't occurred to me right off. But I couldn't think of anyone else.

I went to Tommy's house Sunday morning without calling. Stopping by his house, I thought, might remind him of the time I dropped off the rules for the Law Review competition. Besides, I didn't want to give him too much time to think about his answer. After all, it could be embarrassing to have a tape recorder in class. The people around him would likely say something. The professor might even say something.

Tommy's wife, Miko, answered the door, still in her robe. Tommy had evidently been getting ready to do some school work when I knocked. On the table next to the Sunday newspaper and his cup of coffee was a pile of pages bound by an industrial-sized paperclip, either an outline or his secured transactions paper. It turned out to be his secured transactions paper.

"I knew you must be winding up," I said. "I saw Jonathan Friday. He was trotting off to turn in his paper."

"He turned in his paper?"

"I suppose. I saw it in the back seat of his car. We decided the papers were so long, a strong opening and closing were crucial. Are you going to polish yours up for the Law Review?"

"That's what I'm going to do over break," he said. "There's no way I'm starting from scratch."

"What're you going to do, add some sections?"

"There are two sections I'll add," he said. "I can use the basic research and construct what's essentially a new paper."

"Are you going to ask if it's okay?"

"I'm not going to ask."

Miko was staring at the newspaper.

"Let me tell you why I've come," I said. "I'm going to Ohio this afternoon. I've got a job interview in Cleveland. I'll arrive in Columbus at one in the morning, drive to Cleveland a few hours later, drive back in the afternoon and be back in New Orleans by around midnight tomorrow night. It's a real pain in the rear. I'm sure I won't get the job, but I have to try. I'm sort of caught. You're in both my Monday classes. I'd really appreciate it if you'd tape Evidence and Business for me."

"No problem."

Miko stared at the Sunday paper.

"It's the last Evidence class," I said. "I hate missing class. I wouldn't ask if there was any other way, but I sort of feel like I have to go. It's a real pain."

"It's the last Evidence class?"

"I don't think we meet on Friday."

"We don't meet on Friday?"

"I don't think so."

December 2
(Monday)

On Monday morning, I was standing in the 26th floor lobby of Fielding & Watt in Cleveland, Ohio. "Just make yourself comfortable," a receptionist told me. "Claudette will be with you shortly."

I asked for directions to the restroom. It was spotless. Framed etchings of ships hung on the walls. Blue water stood in the urinals and in the toilet bowl. The spickets shined.

When I returned to the lobby, I looked through one of the firm's brochures stacked conspicuously on a coffee table. The description of the firm's environmental practice was laden with scientific terminology, much of it information about the firm's ability to conduct environmental audits, the scientific end of the environmental law spectrum.

Claudette came out to greet me, making the usual apologies. They lead a busy life, these recruiting coordinators. We sat down in her office. My morning, she explained, would be made up of a series of twenty-minute interviews. I would be escorted from office to office by one of the associates, Bob Paxton, a graduate of Bowling Green State University and the University of Toledo Law School. After receiving his law degree in 1985, he spent several years with Housing and Urban Development in Washington, D.C.

My only strategy for the morning was to talk about anything but law. That was my conclusion from the Gaines interviews. I was convinced that anyone could ask a series of questions about the firm. But the firm doesn't have to sell itself to students. For $70,000 a year, most law students would spend ten hours a day in a sensory deprivation tank. I had the ability. If they thought differently I wouldn't be sitting in their offices, taking up their time. The best a prospective clerk could do was to come across as a likable person, someone with whom the people at the firm would enjoy working. So I spent most of the first interview, with a former Big Ten football tackle, talking about the great riverboat trip down the Mississippi to New Orleans, a trip neither of us had taken.

I next met with Jerome Thorson, the chairman of the Recruiting Committee. He was standing on a stool behind his desk watering plants on his bookshelf when I was ushered into his office. He stood there, a lumpy man with baggy tan slacks and crumpled white shirt, slightly hunched, frozen for a moment as if he had been caught making obscene telephone calls. Bob and I waited as he gathered enough balance to step from his perch without toppling over. The situation sparked a certain intimacy. This was Jerome Thorson, chairman of the Recruiting Committee, a pushover, a flower.

"I'm trying to water the plants more," he explained once he got down. "The plants in the office usually die from inattention."

He was a daisy.

Harry Canton, the environmental lawyer to whom I had written to get the interview, was out of town. I met instead with another of the firm's environmental lawyers, a less interested audience perhaps.

"So how do you know Fay Rubenstein?" he asked me right off.

"She works with my uncle," I told him.

He nodded. "How did you get interested in environmental law?"

I went into what by now was my standard response. When I was at Ohio State, I helped to start a newsletter called the *Solid Waste Reporter*. I had been looking for a part-time job, any part-time job, when the offer came along. I did the work, conducted the interviews, attended seminars, became interested.... That was my story. But I wanted to give something more. How did I become interested? *Pollution should offend you ... like sticking a cork up a mule's ass ... inevitable loopholes ...* I pointed to the glass of water on his desk. "I guess I was just interested in what the heck was in my drinking water," I said, finally.

He nodded politely. "Do you think you can represent industry?" he asked.

I smiled. He had a copy of Rachel Carson's *Silent Spring* on his bookshelf, the book that had almost single-handedly ushered in the environmental movement. "This is a field with good points on both sides," I said, holding out my palms as if they were scales of justice. "Both sides are important to sort of balance things out. Industry is responsible for our high standard of living, but environmentalists are necessary to provide some checks. That's why I think I became interested in environmental law."

He nodded.

Even I was bored.

So I went from one interview to the next, deflecting questions, trying to figure out in the first five minutes what motivated these men and women, and in the process becoming more and more dissatisfied, more and more uncertain, more and more weary with each smile, each shake of the hand.

Any goodwill I had built up disintegrated in the office of Mr. Trevor T. Osting, a graduate of the University of Michigan Law School and hopeless Wolverine football fan. On the top shelf behind him was a glazed crumpled University of Michigan beer mug. Ohio State football team had just lost to Michigan in the Big Ten season finale the week before, a game I hadn't seen, and too soon into the interview an awkward silence fell between us.

"You look busy," I said, referring to the mound of papers on his desk.

"Yeah."

"You do corporate work?"

He started to tell me how much he enjoyed his work, but quickly tired of the subject and turned to me. "Can I answer any of your questions?"

I was taken by surprise. I had no questions left to ask. None. I had asked all of my questions earlier in the day. "Everyone's been real good about answering my questions," I said, thinking, thinking. "Well, I don't know if I should ask, but, well, I guess I'd find out anyway…. Does the firm have any skeletons in the closet?"

Dumb question. Dumb. Why would I want to remind him that I, the nephew of a big client, would be privy to firm gossip? But just when I thought I was caught and squirming, I noticed that Mr. Trevor T. Osting seemed to be a bit uncomfortable himself.

"I don't know," he said. "Let me think. No one's asked me that before…. I guess they were probably just too scared."

"As a clerk, you learn all the gossip anyway."

Why would I want to give him the idea that I sat around on the job swapping the latest gossip, that I would be interested in such things, that I might repeat such things? To my disappointment, he thought the question through.

"No," he said. "I can't think of anything scandalous ever happening at this firm."

No associates falsifying time sheets for their secretaries? No commingling of client funds? No cover-ups? No missed filing deadlines? No hanky panky behind office doors?

Certainly not.

Things didn't get better. I made a mistake about the number of children he had, although a large picture of his three children was right next to his desk, and when I asked him if he socialized with other associates, he said, "First of all, I'm a partner."

"I'm sorry."

"I've been a partner for four years."

It wasn't the blunder of the year, but it was bad. Trevor T. Osting looked young enough to be an associate, his hair a mass of tight blond curls, and he was obviously sensitive about it. Worse, the question, in retrospect, didn't even appear to make much sense. In general, people socialize with their neighbors, people from school or from church. If he didn't socialize with other members of the firm, it wouldn't be something he would want to discuss. If he did, perhaps he was involved in a situation into which I had no business sticking my nose. Did he socialize with the members of the firm? His answer came out pretty flat: "No."

I made a pitiful effort to bring the conversation back around to football. Fortunately, Bob Paxton appeared in the doorway.

"Has it been twenty minutes already?" Trevor Osting asked.

"By my watch," Bob said.

"Seems like we just sat down."

"It's hard to get to know someone when you spend all your time talking about football," Bob said.

Instead of what really mattered? Did he think we'd been talking about football the whole time? Were my reviews already coming in? *Nice guy, but hard to know what he's really like when all we talked about was riverboat gambling and vacation disasters.... Not sure he's committed to the law, let alone this firm.*

I stood up. We all stood over his desk. That desk. The mound of papers. It was all I could see. A large executive desk of thick wood that curled like paisley. Piles of papers everywhere. I must have said something because Bob said, "I bet he can find what he needs in a minute." I only wanted an explanation of what he did each day, what it was like to sit at that desk, make the decisions he made, know the things he knew. I wanted to know how he had become a success, how he had come to sit on the other side of that thick piece of wood in this tall building in this sprawling city. His thoughts were scattered across the desk. His life was in shambles. His wife had left him and taken the kids. He was sleeping with one of the women in accounts receivable. But he was a lawyer, and

I had no idea, really, what it was like to be a lawyer. I also had serious doubts about ever finding out.

*   *   *

Lunch was with Bob and two other associates, Ann and Frederick. Ann practiced securities law, and Frederick worked in the environmental law section, making him the one I would have to impress.

"You worked at Gaines last summer?" he asked. He likely knew some of the people there. Before joining Fielding he had worked in the state attorney general's office in Columbus.

"That's right."

"Did you interview with them for next summer?"

"Yes, I did."

"And they didn't make you an offer?"

"I haven't heard yet," I told him.

His expression reflected perfectly my own frustration. Hadn't heard yet! It was December! He could see immediately that they were playing games down there. Here I was back in Ohio, still interviewing, trying to pull more strings, little strings, tiny little strings that would get me lunch if I made a thousand-mile flight at my own expense, lunch but no reimbursement on parking. Those people at Gaines. They were the ones on retainer with my uncle's company. They were the ones flaunting their successes all over the Midwest, parlaying one thing into another, growing into a firm to be reckoned with. They were the ones who had to pay the piper. He couldn't believe it. He knew those guys. Same old tricks. His expression said it all. It was the first real satisfaction I'd had all day.

We were sitting in a restaurant in the middle of a mall. The food, Bob said, was supposed to be pretty good. He had been meaning to get over for a long time.... And as they took turns speaking amongst themselves, as my morning wound to a close over kaiser rolls and carrot cake, I found myself tired and edgy and growing moreso by the minute. I had walked onto the stage without any lines, without any direction, and now I stood there too stunned to exit and too stubborn to listen to the advice of my supporting cast. They were going on and on about a nun with a law degree who worked to get prisoners released from a Peruvian jail, one of the worst jails on earth. What were they getting at with this talk? Were they trying to soften the blow? Why this sudden interest in the socially responsible lawyer? I wanted a job like theirs. I wanted to squash environmental wackos. I was ready to sing the praises of the Chemical Age. I ordered the same thing they did, chicken something, and said how good it was. Were they trying to get me to explode in a liberal tirade against the penal system, against making money? Did I look like I didn't fit into their world? Was it something about my background? Was it that I had a year unaccounted for on my resume? Getting a master's degree in English doesn't exactly indicate a person whose first goal in life is to manage a million dollar portfolio. Did they know something of the anti-industry bent of Tulane's environmental law clinic? There was a Tulane graduate at the firm. The chairman of the Recruiting Committee had told me his wife was from New Orleans. Did they know something and what exactly did they know?

Frederick didn't seem to have a clue, either. "I've bought a house," he said, buttering his roll.

They were surprised.

"It's in blah blah across the blah blah ..."

It was an odd moment to make the announcement. I decided that these people didn't know each other very well. Funny how recruiting can bring associates together.

We finished eating and walked outside into a drizzle. We said our goodbyes under the overhang of their office building. I tried to make a special effort with Frederick. His lips had turned almost white. He shook my hand and gave me a word or two of encouragement, but they were just words, lost in the mist. Only his lips were moving.

Then I was back in my mother's car heading south again. In two hours, I would be back in Columbus. I had already flown a thousand miles, would end up driving three hundred more. I had the long flight back still ahead. I was tired, badgered, bitter. As soon as I got onto I-71, it hit me how tired I was. But I had at least managed to keep my suit reasonably dry. I combed my hair, poured some coffee from the thermos mom had sent along, reclined the chair a little and fiddled with the radio until I found a familiar song.

*   *   *

Back in Columbus, I parked and was in the basement of the Payback Building with twenty minutes to spare. It was almost over, my day. I was looking forward to dinner with my parents. Within a few hours, I'd be back in New Orleans.

I walked through a maze of tunnels, found the bathroom, checked my hair. It was still damp. I combed it back from my forehead more than I usually did. I thought I looked a little older and left feeling a little more confident. I had seen a pay phone on the way in, and I stopped to call Katie.

"Any news?" I asked.

She wanted to know how the interviews had gone. She didn't understand immediately that I was interested in whether Gaines had called.

"The woman from the EPA called," she said.

"Really? That sounds good."

"What does she want?"

"I don't know. I just talked to her the other day. Maybe she got my resume from the director and wants to offer me a job."

"That'd be nice."

Katie liked the idea of Washington. More and more, the idea seemed to be settling well with her. No doubt, we would have some fun. There were beaches nearby, plenty to see. Katie knew people who lived just outside of the city, friends of her family, about our age, she said. She didn't seem to worry that I'd be making no money, that the cost of living would all but kill us.

*   *   *

The lobby of the venerable Branegan, Reed, Dowd & Spatz reminded me of a casino. I thought of the old Showboat on the boardwalk in Atlantic City. Both had carpeting the same shade of orange. The receptionist sat behind her high desk with a bored expression as if she were about to deal a hand of blackjack.

From the lobby I could look down through tinted glass on the Capitol Building. I stood at the edge and looked at the atrium in the lobby several floors below and the trees that seemed to flourish there. In a conference room on a lower floor, a young fellow had spread papers across the table and was writing onto a yellow pad.

The receptionist once again offered me a seat, but I decided to remain standing. I thought standing made a better impression. It was easier to move forward and shake hands from a stance. I would avoid that awkwardness of having the interviewer waiting for me to clumsily rise, grab my coat and writing sample, stick out my hand and smile and look somehow graceful while trying to give the impression that I belonged. By standing I would never have to take my eyes off the interviewer. And I could convey an impression of one who was energetic, on the go, a person whose time was important.

I had been standing already for close to half an hour. A man hurriedly walked back and forth across the hallway several times, and I did my best to feign interest in the parchment documents encased in glass on the walls that seemed to have some relation to the establishment of counties in the state.

Down the hall, I could see through an open door part of an office. The view of the Olentangy River from there was probably splendid, the factories, and further, the land that had beckoned people westward. First there was just some motion in the office, an arm reaching across the desk. Then I saw the fellow who occupied it. He appeared in the doorway. He was enormous. I thought he looked fierce. A rotund man with a huge head and beard and bushy eyebrows who would as soon break me in two as look at me. When you're young and overweight you get whipcream sprayed on your head the last day of school. When you're older, you scare the hell out of them, all of them. They don't even know why they're scared, but you do. You feel their fear. It makes you stronger. It makes you bigger. It makes you better. It gives you power ...

I was using my last bit of strength to remain standing. Perhaps I thought if I sat down I'd never get up. The sofa seemed small and far away. When the recruiting coordinator finally appeared, tossing off apologies and leading me once again to the edge, I did my best to manage enthusiasm for the view.

"I see some people have found a nice place to work," I said, nodding toward the man who would be up all night.

Her voice was a whisper, and she whispered through the hall, through our tour of the library, all the way to her office. Although I stared at her, dumbfounded, I couldn't get her to stop whispering. Lawyers occasionally talk in subdued tones, and such tones are easily mistaken as the hallmark of professionalism. Sitting in her small windowless office, my voice grew louder as I spoke. I wanted passion. I wanted life. I wanted a cheer, a scream, a human sacrifice even if it had to be me. How could she not go completely crazy in her tiny office? It was a broom closet. It was stifling. At least she could have done a dance on her little desk. Instead, she asked me whether I considered any undergraduate schools other than Ohio State and to what other law schools I had been accepted. The old search for the intelligence quotient, I thought. Branegan, Reed, Dowd & Spatz well knew that someone could get good grades working twelve hours a day. Could someone get good grades working four hours a day? An average person can work like a mule and perhaps get a job at a large firm. To make partner, the hours may very well be horrendous. Great grades may get you noticed, but great grades and law review … and a full-time job … and a family … these things say you can perform a juggling act. Law firms don't necessarily want you to have a coronary at eleven at night in their library.

The recruiting coordinator evidently had the impression that her job was to find very smart lawyers. I mentioned a few second-flight schools and, from a pile of firm material atop her filing cabinet, she gave me a brochure that featured the firm's interior decorating. I opened the glossy magazine to a centerfold of a conference table with champagne on ice and shining crystal glasses waiting to be toasted.

"I always thought the smartest person at a law firm is the recruiting coordinator," I told her.

She made several calls to Neil Benetton, chairman of the firm's Hiring Committee. Finally he was ready to see me. He turned out to be the fellow I had seen rushing back and forth in the hallway. It was dark now outside and his window had become a mirror. The mirror effect helped to avoid, I supposed, that terribly depressing feeling that another day has passed behind a desk and the day was still far from over. My day was still far from over. I needed a hot shower. I started to wonder if I would even have time for dinner.

"I like to ask people to tell me about themselves," he said.

I raised my eyebrows. The recruiting coordinator had asked me to do this very thing only minutes before. I didn't mind giving the impression that I found the request a little ridiculous.

He went on, "Tell me of the significant events in your life, that sort of thing, so I can get an idea of who you are. I've tried different ways of interviewing people over the years, and I've found that helpful.… Someday, if I can find the time, I'm going to write a book about recruiting and sell it to law students and make a million dollars and retire."

Okay. He was already a millionaire. I once read about a lawyer at Branegan who owned a collection of Rolls Royces. The guy had dozens of Rolls Royces. Come to think of it, he had looked like a pretty portly fellow as well. Now I had to think: What would a millionaire want to hear from me, a second-year law student tens of thousands of dollars in debt that would make him, the millionaire, want to cast his magic wand over my head?

"Well, I was born in an army hospital in Nurnburg, Germany. The year was 1968.... Shall I continue?" I was trying to have a little fun.

"Please do," he said.

"My father was in the service. My uncle had been in the same branch."

"Is your uncle someone I should know?" he said.

"No, not really."

I hit the highlights of my resume. My life. I wouldn't be deterred. I had rehearsed my story a number of times before, usually in pieces. Now I was just putting some of the pieces together. When an interesting tangent arrived, I took it. Perhaps he would find it interesting that I had been on the high school golf team, that we had won the Central Catholic League championship, that I was married, that I kept up my interest in coin collecting by buying proof sets every year.

"Where were we?" I asked. We both attempted to find where I had left off. As an undergraduate, I worked on the school newspaper. In graduate school, I worked with one of the giants in the field of rhetoric and composition.

"Law school is probably a lot different from studying English," he said.

"Not really," I said, sticking to my impression that the two courses of study were quite similar. "You have to make sense of a line of cases."

After I finished, it was his turn to talk. "I think the greatest asset a lawyer can have is to be trustworthy," he said. "There are a lot of smart lawyers out there, but there are few who are really trustworthy."

Now I was trying to figure things out. He tried to help me. He told me that all of the offers for the summer program had been made and that they were waiting to see who would accept. I looked at myself in the mirrored glass. It was late, but it was hard to say how late.

*   *   *

I didn't have time for dinner. Dad gave me a copy of the *Columbus Bar Association Journal* to read on the plane. There was an article in it by James Cole, my friend at Gaines, on literary references to lawyers. He explained that the passage in Shakespeare's *Henry VI* containing the line about killing all the lawyers is, when taken in context, actually quite complimentary of lawyers. The *Journal* also contained an article by Philip Korovin, the hiring partner at Folger, Hines, whose letter I had tacked to my refrigerator with the word "OOPS!" He was writing about the job market. It was bad out there, he admitted. He was sorry that his firm couldn't hire everyone who walked through the door. The students he met were all bright, qualified. They would all make excellent attorneys. They had all overcome some obstacle to get to where they were, at the top of a group of overachievers. It broke his heart to see them come and go, bright smiles and firm handshakes. They must teach that handshake in law school, he joked.

It was an article full of the bleary-eyed whimsy of an old man recalling the French girl he had left behind after the War. What he didn't say was how the choices were made, how the lucky were chosen. He couldn't just come out and say that no one in his right mind would bring his girlfriend home when he had his high school sweetheart waiting at the dock.

*   *   *

It was after midnight when I shuffled upstairs to my apartment. With what seemed like my last effort, I hung my suit on the door, dropped into a chair, and, when Katie set a microwave dinner on the card table in front of me, scalded the roof of my mouth on apple fritters.

15

"You're the second person who's told me that," Jonathan said when I told him there was no Evidence class on Friday.

As it turned out, I was wrong. We did have class on Friday. Where I had gotten the idea otherwise I could only guess. Wishful thinking, perhaps. But we had class Friday, and my first exam, B.E., was on Monday. I would have only two days to study. Two days. I experienced one of those sensations that reminded me I was really in law school, where some get ahead and others are left behind. The thought was sickening.

Jonathan and I were in the lounge talking. By the time Tommy came in, our talk had drifted to Pollution Control, and we were trying to figure out what obscure point Muder would include on the exam. Something she had only touched upon in class, we figured, perhaps even something not discussed at all, a footnote from one of the assigned cases.

"Muder included mixing zones on last year's exam," Jonathan said.

"Mixing zones?"

"Wasn't math taken off the LSAT sometime in the seventies," Tommy said.

Mixing zones? What else was fair game? We all had to wonder. What wasn't context and opinion and poetry was, presumably, the material over which we would be tested. But Muder was unusual in that she hadn't spent class time dwelling on cases or holdings. Her approach seemed, in retrospect, to give us a sense of the landscape, hence the field trips, the slide presentations, the participatory exercises. She gave us context and background and opinion. A lot of opinion.

I had been counting heavily on my class notes, which I had begun to review the night before. Instead of coming to life, though, the notes had just lain there like pieces of flesh and scattered bones. Muder had left the task of assembling the course to us. It was becoming clear that Pollution Control was one of those courses where I should have read the assigned material closely and put it together on my own. Muder wasn't one to give anything away. She wouldn't do the bulk of our work for us. Why had it taken me so long to figure this out? I had been too busy to give the material the kind of reading she required. Worse, no good commercial study aids existed for the course. I had bought the Nutshell on environmental law but found it didn't go into depth on the topics Muder covered in class. Environmental law was too amorphous a topic. I was marketing myself as a future environmental lawyer, and I was at risk of failing my first environmental law class. I had my class notes, sure, but they were already attracting buzzards.

"I have your tapes," Tommy said.

"Thanks. Thanks a lot. Any problems?"

He shook his head as he pulled my recorder from his bookbag. I turned on the tape and listened. Landrow's voice was harder to make out than I had hoped.

"Try playing it on the stereo," Tommy suggested.

"Okay. Did Landrow write anything useful on the board?"

"You want my notes?"

He gave me his notes from Evidence and B.E., and I eagerly accepted.

*   *   *

CERCLA operates on the proposition that those who have had control of a waste site should help to clean it up. And with joint and several liability, the net of CERCLA liability is deep as well as wide. To give us an idea of this liability, Muder posed a hypothetical:

Suppose we have a lake owned by Louisiana State University (LSU) containing old batteries and oil. The batteries, manufactured by Chemical Co. and Captain Electric, are dumped on its bank and contain PCBs. They were sold by King Hardware. Some were taken to the lake by Waste Control Corp. under contract with LSU. Ninety percent of the oil was dumped by Super Oil of Louisiana, which has since merged with Exxon. Ten percent was dumped by Pittston, a company now in bankruptcy. There are two tracts of land which contain part of the bank. One, where the batteries are dumped, is owned by LSU. It was given to LSU by a booster. The land is rented to Waste Control and insured by Aetna. The other tract is owned by Donald Trump, whose note has been assumed by First National Bank. The bank has put a fence around the property and proclaimed it to be under bank management.

"The lawyer who made that decision is now looking for a new job," Muder said, to much amusement. "Who's in? Who's out? What is the standard of proof? Who can sue?"

We would spend the next two days going over the lake hypo. Almost everyone was liable. "I know of one law firm held liable because an associate told the client not to worry about abandoning a site," Muder told us, as an aside. "The law firm was held to be an aider and abettor of waste disposal."

The class groaned.

Before class ended, Muder announced an optional review session Thursday after class from 3:45 to 4:30. Students were asking questions in her office, she said, and her answers might give some an unfair advantage. Instead, she would hold one review session and all questions would be brought at that time. Any question was fair provided (1) it was first asked to at least one other student before the session and (2) it was presented in writing 24 hours before the session.

I hurried home after class to call Joslyn Fink at the EPA before she left for the day. As it turned out, Joslyn had called me by mistake. She was returning a message I had left on her answering machine several days before, an earlier attempt of mine to reach her.

"Didn't you say you went to Vanderbilt?" she asked.

"No ... I thought you might have gotten my resume from Mr. English," I said. I didn't mind reminding her that the EPA already had a copy of my resume floating around.

"No."

I repeated my interest in working for the EPA and promised, once again, to send my resume to her.

A job with the EPA would be good, but I certainly didn't have the same view of the EPA I once did. Like most Americans, I suppose, I had thought the EPA always fought to protect the environment. I was astounded by the number of cases we read in class where environmental groups had sued the EPA to act in the best interest of the environment. In one case we read, the EPA had even fought a requirement to use recycled paper. Still, working for the EPA didn't shut any doors. Industry didn't mind seeing it on your resume. I would get to Joslyn's letter that night, I figured, when I sat down to write thank you notes to each of the lawyers I had met at Fielding and Branegan.

*　　*　　*

That evening, after I finished the last of the thank you letters, I listened to the tapes Tommy had made. Landrow had finished our discussion on experts and gone through privileges: lawyer-client, doctor-patient, priest-penitent, husband-wife. Some people because of their positions could not be forced to testify under certain circumstances. These privileges were pretty self-explanatory and well described in Emanuel's.

I put in the other tape and listened to Tarenzella.

"That's your professor?" Katie asked.

I nodded, looking up as Tarenzella continued to shriek. I had to smile. I had gotten used to the stridency of Tarenzella's voice, but Katie reminded me that she was a professor out of control, shrieking for her life.

Tarenzella was trying to start her lecture, but someone had apparently asked about the exam. "This was settled a long time ago," she said. "You can bring your statute, but it is not an open-book exam. I've said this now several times. Now let's get on with class."

To my knowledge, this was the first time she had made such an announcement, unless something was said on a day I had missed. I didn't think so. I imagined she just heard the question so often during office hours she thought by now everyone knew her answer.

We were talking about piercing the corporate veil, what Tarenzella called "PCV," the process of breaking the limited liability of the corporate entity. I listened to the tape and followed along with Tommy's notes, adding material in the margin where appropriate. Generally speaking, one could pierce the corporate veil and sue a parent corporation in three instances: when a subsidiary is under the complete dominion of the parent; when a corporation has completely disregarded the usual trimmings of a corporate entity, such as meetings and minutes; or when a corporation is severely undercapitalized. In stronger cases, more than one of these elements is present. One case we read listed nineteen factors that helped the court decide to PCV.

As the tape approached the end of the first side, I became a little anxious. I was almost to the end of Tommy's notes, and there had to be at least another half-hour left in the class. I flipped the tape to the other side. A few minutes later there was a click and then hiss. I looked at the tape. The reels were still rolling, the tape still feeding. No words. Hiss. Almost thirty minutes were missing, and the last line at the bottom of Tommy's notes was the last thing Tarenzella had said on the tape.

December 4
(Wednesday)

I ran into Howard Sloan, my 1L neighbor from across the hall, making copies of old exams. Like most schools, Tulane keeps copies of past exams on file. It's good practice, many believe, to go over past exams. Sometimes the questions from year to year are very similar. Often the issues haven't changed. Many students try to finish their outlines two weeks before the end of the semester and spend the final two weeks working old exams in study groups. During my first semester I looked at a couple of old exams and found them of little use. They merely told me what I already knew, that I had to study more. Since then, I generally avoided them altogether and spent my time studying. I was always studying up to the very last minute.

"You getting some old exams?" I asked him.

"Are they a good idea?" he wanted to know. He always asked my advice. He was a good kid.

"It's not a bad idea," I said.

Howard didn't look real good. His smile was uncertain.

"What do you have there?" I asked.

"Torts. Bonfante."

"I had Bonfante," I said, dropping my voice to a whisper. I was going to give him some advice, some good advice. "On his exam, on his instructions, he writes that he doesn't care if you spot every issue, he just wants to see what you can do with an issue. He wants to see some legal analysis. I only figured out this summer what he wants. It just suddenly hit me when I was working on a torts problem at the law firm I was at. You know the different theories of causation, the indeterminate defendant issues, alternative liability theories, you know, like market share liability, enterprise liability, that sort of stuff. Take them and apply them to any situation. I figured it all out this summer. Whenever there's an injury, there are any number of people who might be responsible. In

Bonfante's book, everyone's potentially liable. That's the way he teaches the course. Whenever there's an injury, there are any number of contributing factors. Apply the different alternative liability theories. Drag everyone in. Everyone. You'll get an A in the course."

"Did you get an A?"

"I did all right, but I only figured out what he wanted this summer."

It was good advice. It just hit me one day at Simoneaux: The net of liability was ever-extending. Bonfante himself often described the huge money judgments he won for severely injured clients on threadbare theories. If someone is injured, Bonfante had frequently told us, it was reasonably foreseeable.

*   *   *

The rest of that afternoon I spent reviewing my Remedies notes, where I found that on October 1st I had scribbled across the top of the page: "Laycock article on reserve." This notation surprised me. Douglas Laycock was the author of our casebook. I had completely forgotten about the article, hadn't given it a second thought. Weeks had passed. Finding the note was almost a shock. My recollection was that Worth had recommended the article highly. After all, it was written by the author of our casebook. Worth had put it on reserve in the library. And the irreparable injury rule was at the heart of many of our classroom discussions, the life blood of much of the course. Perhaps Worth's intonation had made me make the note to look at the article in my spare time. And I had forgotten about it completely.

I went to the front desk of the library and looked at the article with a growing sense of excitement. I could tell from the first page—the outline, the cases cited—that the article would give a large section of the course some unity. For the moment, it seemed as if my problems were solved. I would outline the article and note a number of insightful things to say on the exam. I was set. But who else would get ahold of the article? How many people were in class the day Worth recommended it? How many people had noted that the article was on reserve, thought it would be of any use? How many didn't care or just plain forgot? The odds were good that only a handful of people would even look at the article. And fewer still would be able to put the article into a form useful for answering some of the questions sure to come up on the exam.

*   *   *

I picked up the telephone in the kitchen and listened. "Kenneth Westphal?" It was a woman's voice. It was the second time she had said my name.

"Yes."

She paused. "Do you have an interview today with Willey, Craig & Greene?"

"Oh my gosh ..." I looked at my watch. It was five-fifteen. I had completely forgotten about the interview in Metairie.

She laughed. "That's okay."

"I'm awfully sorry about this."

"When can you come in?"

"You mean you still want to speak with me?"

"Of course," she said. "It could happen to anybody."

We rescheduled the interview for the following Monday at the same time.

I hung up and told Katie. "I missed the interview."

She took it personally. "I should have put a note on the refrigerator."

"That wasn't the problem. I can't keep anything straight these days. I completely forgot about it. They want me to go in Monday."

Katie thought about this.

"Do you think I should cancel?" I said. "It would just be a waste of time, wouldn't it?"

Katie seemed to agree.

"That's what I think."

Monday morning I called and told the receptionist that I had an interview with one of the Hiring Committee members at five o'clock. I wouldn't be able to make it.

"Would you like to reschedule?" she asked.

"No," I said. "I'll explain with a letter."

"Do you think it was with Mr. Price?" she asked.

"That sounds right."

I sat down and wrote a letter saying how sorry I was to have missed the interview. This was an insurance firm, I told myself, trying not to feel too badly about the mistake. It was in Metairie. Besides, I wouldn't have gotten the job anyway. That was really my attitude. More than any berating by a professor or a mediocre performance on a law school exam, the process of interviewing was telling me, louder and louder, that I didn't have what it takes to be a lawyer. I was being whittled away, the chips were flying, and I wondered if I would ever be whole again.

16

As I reviewed for the B.E. exam, I realized that I was still missing notes from the day I interviewed with the Compadre Club and Hanssen, Hess. In one day, Tarenzella had covered 100 pages on limited partnerships, so I began to wonder who in the class might be able to help. It occurred to me after some thought that I might get the notes from Trent Hebert. He sat a few rows behind me. We had been in the same writing group our first semester and had finished a library research project in record time. We still said hello in the halls. I left a note in his folder:

> Trent—
> I noticed that you are in my B.E. class w/ Tarenzella. I am missing one day's notes & wondered if you could give me a copy of yours for that day—the last day she discussed limited partnerships & began corporations. It was a terrible day to miss. She flew through 100 pages.
> Needless to say, if you have missed any days in B.E., please let me know.
> Just drop it in my folder if you can.
> Thanks,
> Ken

I spent the rest of the morning preparing an injunction Worth had assigned for class. He had hinted that he would collect them, and had given the impression that we might be asked to write an injunction on the exam. But in class that afternoon, rather than collect them, he distributed a model answer he had drafted.

"I'm not going to collect them," he said, when someone asked. "Of course, I'd be happy to provide comments on an individual basis." Then he launched into a quick review of the course: Where there is a wrong, ask what are the appropriate remedies; generally, this means asking what is the plaintiff's rightful position ...

I went up after class to show him my injunction, the only person, apparently, to take him up on his offer, but I thought I had written a pretty good one, better even, perhaps, than the one he had distributed to the class. My heart sank when, after glancing at it, he stuck it in his folder with his class notes. I had just wanted a quick response, a pat on the back, some kind word. Instead, I found myself following him down the hall to his office. Once there, he still didn't seem to have any interest in looking at my injunction. He said he would review it and call me with comments.

The injunction was only one page long!

But I gave him my phone number. He wrote it down on a pink square of paper and said he would give me a call after he'd had time to review it.

On my way out of the building, I saw Jose in the lounge laughing with a group of students. He had gone through the entire course of Remedies without being called on. I had heard, though, that he had been the center of attention almost every day in Professor Niedenthal's Negotiable Instruments class. Niedenthal was one of the more traditional professors at Tulane. He taught by the book, a dusty old book that cast professors in the role of stern father. Three days a week, Niedenthal had probed the mind of Jose Cadicamo, getting him used to attention, used to thinking under pressure, used to the warm flush of his own face. Jose had told the same story to both Worth and Niedenthal, I imagined, something about his job and other commitments. He told them he would have trouble being prepared every day; Worth and Niedenthal just had different ideas about the role of law professor.

*   *   *

Muder spent the last class going over the lake hypo. She didn't save time for any final words of wisdom. She distributed evaluations and said, "These don't tell me how I did. The exams tell me how I did."

No doubt she had high hopes for the class, filled as it was with people dedicated to environmental law, people who had been working in the environmental law clinic, people on the ELJ, people pursuing a master's degree in Environmental Law Studies. No doubt she was looking forward to reading these exams.

I stood a good chance of being beaten to a pulp by the grading curve. Most of the practicing attorneys had tape recorded the class lectures and recently a few had shown up in class with thick transcripts prepared by their secretaries. I would write my exam in fountain pen and hope Muder mistook me for one of the practicing attorneys. She would have to give me at least a passing grade; those guys came to class every day and even asked questions.

Most of the class stayed for the review session. I was hoping to learn something as well. The day before, I had left in Muder's mailbox a question about Air Quality Control Regions, the subject she covered when I was in Columbus interviewing with Gaines:

> **Prof. Muder:**
> **Could you please go over the material concerning Air Quality Control Regions. You said it was the toughest material we covered all semester. We believe it.**
> **Thank you.**
> **Concerned Students**

It was written on yellow paper, neatly printed, and I watched to see how Muder would handle it.

The problem with a question and answer session is that students probe minuscule points, points which may provide some sense of ease to the person asking the question but which inevitably increase the anxiety of everyone else. Where do these questions come from? Who knows the answer to that? We turned to one another with raised eyebrows as the questions were read.

Soon after she started, people began to leave. This was typical. Most people don't like review sessions but feel obligated to attend, at least long enough to get the general tenor. The questions were inane, arcane, insane. Panic was setting in. The time was better spent studying. Some stayed because they were afraid of missing anything. Others just stayed because they were afraid.

Muder looked at the yellow paper in her hand and shook her head. She read the question out loud. "We spent an entire class period on this," she said. "This is neither the time nor the place to go over this now. Remember, I put it all on the board ..." She was looking at the blackboard. It seemed for a moment as if she were having second thoughts, as if she might go ahead and provide a brief synopsis or hit the highlights.

She didn't.

Jonathan looked at me out of the corner of his eye. I always took notes on yellow paper.

December 6
(Friday)

I found a handwritten note from Trent in my folder:

> I too am missing notes from 10/30—sorry I can't help—if you need any other notes let me know and I'll see what I can do. (I could have the wrong day, you might want to check. I have the notes for 11/4 if that is what you're after.)

So, I thought, that's that. I would go into the exam without knowing what Tarenzella had said about limited partnerships, and there was no way I'd have time to read the material.

*   *   *

Unlike Muder, unlike every other professor I'd had at law school, Landrow didn't leave the room as we completed our evaluations. He leaned against the table at the front, glancing at his notes much as he had on the first day of class, keeping things under control. At the back of the room, though, out of earshot, the general consensus of students was that he was too cocky. That was what Sharon wrote on her evaluation. She laughed, and others agreed.

"Listen up," Landrow said. "we haven't yet gone over the exam. I have a slightly different way of grading."

That brought the class to order.

We passed forward our evaluations, and he set forth his scheme: The exam would be 60 percent multiple-choice and 40 percent traditional essay. The multiple-choice was unusual. He called it multiple multiple-choice. Each question could have one, two, three, four, or five correct answers. Or it might have no correct answer at all, in which case we were to leave the answer spaces blank. Multiple multiple-choice.

While essay exams are still by far the most common way to test students, many professors come up with ways to make their grading a little easier, especially in large classes. Some professors put space limitations on the answer. Others make at least part of the exam multiple-choice.

The year before, Bonfante, my torts professor, wanted to write an exam made up entirely of multiple-choice and true-false questions. "There are an awful lot of you people," he said, "and that means a lot of exams to grade, so I'm reserving the right to give a multiple-choice exam. Some people like them and some don't.... I like them." As the semester wore on, he seemed to like the idea more and more. A week before finals, he distributed a couple of sample questions:

Is stupidity an excuse for not acting as a reasonable person under the circumstances?

A commercial airline crashes in the ocean. There is testimony that the pilot was drunk. Is this an appropriate case for the doctrine of *res ipsa loquitor*?

The questions created a certain tension among students, especially as we began to go over the answers. What's the answer to the second one, then?... Huh? Bonfante would look up in amazement that everyone didn't see that *res ipsa* is only needed when there is no direct evidence of negligence.

"That's true," he said.

"It's truly ambiguous," one of the older students replied. He was forty years old and, I suppose, had more at stake than most.

Bonfante looked again at the question. He wasn't defeated, just thinking.

"It's too subjective," the student said to those sitting nearby.

"It's all subjective, anyway," another said under his breath. "Whether it's multiple-choice or essay, it's subjective."

That didn't make the older student feel any better. On an essay exam, his knowledge of the law had room to roam. He could outrun the younger members of the class, earning points just for his carefully phrased issues. But on a multiple-choice exam, anyone could get lucky.

Landrow was trying to be explicit, but the more he told us about the exam, the more we had to wonder about. Sometimes there would be no correct answers. Sometimes there would be more than one correct answer. *Be careful.* We would be pressed for time. We got a point for each correct answer and lost a point for each incorrect answer. Did everyone get that? "The reason," Landrow said, "is to discourage guessing." He spoke of guessing with a certain disgust.

Jeremy leaned over and said the way to take the exam was to be conservative on the multiple-choice and then ace the essay. I nodded, thinking he was probably right. People would somehow mess up the multiple-choice. But what was conservative? What exactly did Landrow mean by a wrong answer?

"Every year," Landrow went on, "somebody asks me, 'Mr. Landrow, do we have to know that Loo-siana law?' Every year. It never fails to amaze me. Do we have to know that Loo-siana law? Okay, all right, any questions about the exam?"

Francis Penwell raised his hand. "Do we have to know that Louisiana law?"

Landrow had a crazy smile on his face. He liked Mr. Penwell.

During the last week of the semester someone always asks the professor if we have to know for the exam some topic or other covered in class. Professor Worth had the best way to answer such questions.

Student:	Do we have to know the collateral bar rule?
Prof. Worth:	No.
Student:	Do we have to know the UCC?
Prof. Worth:	No.

Worth caught on quickly. Students today need to relax. Did they have to know the collateral bar rule? No. Did they have to know most of the things in the casebook? No. They could still pass. It's very hard to fail a law school exam. Why did they even ask? Would it help to know these things? Well, that was another story. That was a different question entirely.

And in the next fifteen minutes, Landrow covered the last chapter of Evidence, what we absolutely had to know about permissive inferences, rebuttable presumptions, conclusive presumptions, adjudicative and legislative facts. My notes that day ended in mid-sentence. Class dismissed. Wild applause.

I went down to speak with Landrow after class. It was the closest I had ever been to him. From the back of the room, he looked much younger, a little man with red hair and mischievous smile. Up close, he conveyed much more authority. Up close he couldn't be challenged. His face showed the long hours of major corporate practice. He had earned his black Corvette. He had a right to his self-confidence, and people who treated him like little Maurice Landrow ran the risk of annihilation.

I was still uncertain about the structure of the exam. A single question could have more than one correct answer, I understood that. But would we lose a point on the question if we didn't get all of the correct answers or would we get points for the three we got correct and then subtract one for missing the fourth correct answer, leaving a net total of two? Some confusing possibilities ricocheted through my mind. I tried to boil them down to one question.

"Can a single question be worth more than one point?" I asked him.

Yes, he said, that was right. "Each question can be worth more than one point."

I looked at him to make sure he knew I was weighing every word he said, and he gave me that smile of his. The guy had perfect teeth.

At home, I dug out the two past Evidence exams I had copied earlier in the semester. The directions for the multiple multiple-choice questions were the same on both:

> Choose the letters for all correct answers and place them in the appropriate space. Unless otherwise noted, assume the federal rules of evidence apply. Write the letters legibly. Do not write notes explaining your answers. The questions do not necessarily have any correct answers. A point will be subtracted for each incorrect entry.

I was temporarily confused again. A point would be subtracted for each incorrect entry. What exactly did that mean? If I answered "C" and the answer was "B," I would, I supposed, lose two points, one for thinking "C" was correct and one for thinking "B" was incorrect. That made some sense. I always had the potential to gain or lose five points. If I'd had the time or inclination, I would have taken consensus responses to old exams and determined the average number of correct answers per question to estimate Landrow's general inclination. If he averaged greater than three correct answers per question, it would be better to guess; if he averaged less than two correct answers, it was better to leave blanks. But I didn't have time, and if I was relying that heavily on statistical irregularities for a law school exam I deserved to be committed.

So I tried to think the problem through. Landrow hated guessing. He had a crazy smile. He would be more likely than most to load his exam with red herrings. Besides, I had trouble imagining him coming up with three correct answers to every question. If this reasoning was correct, each random response would more likely be incorrect than correct. There would always be more to lose than to gain. The best way to proceed would be a conservative approach.

Jeremy had seen it almost immediately. The rewards of guessing just didn't match the risks. That was what Landrow meant by dissuading guessing. He hated guessing. A future patent attorney for Procter & Gamble, Jeremy had seen it almost immediately.

* * *

That afternoon a group of us got together for lunch at The Boot, a bar next to the school. I reluctantly agreed. I'd had some notion of going over my Pollution Control notes again that afternoon before settling down for a weekend of B.E. But I guess I had to eat. Jonathan was there. So were Tommy, Kevin St. Germain, Rosey, Ted. Jose was there, too, which surprised me. I had no idea he was one of the gang. It was the Bar Review Party all over again. Over lunch, I gradually began to understand that it was Jose who had taken over Tommy's job after he made the Law Review. They had evidently been friends, good friends, for some time.

At both ends of the bar on Court TV broadcast the trial of a doctor had been charged with raping one of his patients.

"I heard the victim broke down and cried on the stand," Rosey said.

"That's how the defendant in a rape case can get off," Jonathan said, "cry on the stand."

"The judge halted the trial," Rosey said.

"Really?"

"That's not right," said Ted.

"Sure it is," Jonathan said. "It's prejudicial."

"I hadn't thought of that," Rosey said.

December 7
(Saturday)

Dear Kenneth:

As Hiring Partner for the Firm, I want to thank you for taking the time to interview with us on Monday, December 2.

I regret that we are unable to extend an invitation to you to visit our offices for an additional interview. This year, because of a very successful recruiting season coupled with a high acceptance rate from our previous summer clerk program, we have already reserved our maximum number of offers for second-year summer clerk positions.

We appreciate your interest in Branegan, Reed, Dowd & Spatz, and we wish you the best in your second year of law school.

Sincerely,
BRANEGAN, REED, DOWD &
SPATZ

Neil W. Benetton

NWB/SAW/cak
199/323

17

In the typical law school class, after 37 1/2 hours in the classroom and four or five hundred pages of material, the sole criteria upon which one's grade lies is a single three-hour exam. The first semester this creates a panic. How can a person possibly know everything read for or discussed in class? And the first attempts at exam taking are splashed with legal terminology, phrases thrown down in a rush, rules recited verbatim without application to the facts. If they can just get the law down on paper, students think, they will at least pass. Many first-year exams scarcely hint that the student came to class every day, studied every night, skipped parties, bit fingernails, rose at dawn.... Many students scarcely form a cogent sentence and yet they pass. Only then does it dawn on them that what they learned over the course of the semester can't possibly be tested in three hours and that what they need to know doesn't take weeks to learn.

There's a joke in law school that if you can't learn the course material in three days it's not worth knowing. And if exams can be justified in no other way, they do at least test one's ability to convey a sense of expertise. After all, being a lawyer means continually becoming an expert on different subjects in a short period of time. Your client's business is your business. Law school exams test one's ability to put on an impromptu show.

I don't know why I should have been surprised. Our vegetables are artificially colored, our food flavor-enhanced. On the evening news, the anchorman asks prepared questions to correspondents who give prepared answers. They read their lines from cue cards like actors. Everything is a play, a production put on for the American public. Why should the education of lawyers be any different? Once students learn not to beat themselves, they get through, sometimes even do quite well. It may take a few semesters to learn the tricks, but once they learn, they can really be said to be lawyers. They have the confidence of lawyers. They can take on the world.

But I wasn't yet halfway through law school.

I was still learning …

December 7
(Saturday afternoon)

Tarenzella's review session was to begin at three-thirty. She would go over the exam from the previous fall. I read it through in the library before class with a growing sense of apprehension. I hadn't spotted many issues, but, I told myself, I hadn't really studied yet, either. I still had time to gather the central issues of the course. I just wanted to know the basics, come up with a plan of attack for the major areas of the course. Usually, this would mean diagramming some sort of approach for each potential exam question, but Tarenzella's exam was closed book, so I had to save time for memorization.

Nobody seemed to be sitting in their assigned seats, so I sat in the back row. Tarenzella looked at me for a moment as if she couldn't place my face, then went on with the review. She had other things on her mind. And I sat there listening to her approach to a preincorporation contract issue with vague recollections and the sickening sense that when our exam was set before us we would be facing something completely different.

During the break, Tommy came up to say hello. We both agreed that it had been a long semester.

"Are you still going to use your toxic torts paper for your comment?" I asked him.

"Noreen Nelan-Rafferty just asked me that same thing," he said. "I was sitting in the library when she brought it up. Marie Burnbaum was sitting nearby and said, 'You can't do that. I asked.'"

"What did you say?"

He shrugged.

"Were they trying to trap you?"

"I think Noreen was thinking about doing the same thing."

"Maybe she wanted to stir up trouble. They knew you were around, right? Maybe she wanted to see how you would react with Marie there."

"I don't know if she was being sneaky."

"Well …"

"Women can be sneaky," Tommy finally decided, suddenly breaking into a grin. He liked what he said so much, he said it again: "Women can be sneaky."

*   *   *

When I got home that evening there was a message on my answering machine from Professor Worth. He'd had time, he said, to review my injunction. It was fine. He would be happy to go over it with me. I could return the call at my convenience.

I ate dinner and then called him back.

"As I said," Worth began, relaxing, I imagined, in plaid and khaki, "your injunction is fine. Some areas could be stronger. Of course, that is almost always the case. Drafting an injunction isn't easy. It's often a difficult balancing act, a form of art. You must write the decree with care, being specific about the acts that must be restrained, while avoiding any sense of overreaching. And of course contempt sanctions must be a meaningful possibility …" He went on for a minute or two.

"Very good," I said. "Do we need to discuss it further?"

"I have some papers I've left at the office. You could meet me there."

"Of course I'm interested in your comments," I said, "but you've been very helpful with what you've already told me. So there's really no reason for you to go out of your way, if there was a chance that you could avoid going back to the office this evening …"

"I may let it go until the morning."

"Very good."

We left it at that.

December 8
(Sunday)

The B.E. exam was now only hours away. My notes were better than I had thought. A good law school class will lay out the current state of the law like a map of World War II Europe. You will leave knowing where the wars are being waged, where the mines are buried, which battles might be won or lost in the future and why. You will have a sense as to when it might be useful to retreat and try an old argument or to move onto something else. Tarenzella wasn't the perfect general, but she had evidently streamlined her approach to the essentials. It turned out to be a pretty good class.

The law of agency was one area on which I focused during review. Tarenzella, I decided, would present a situation where the agent acted without the express authority of the principal. We had spent too much time on the subject in class for her to ignore it. I made a list of issues I could address: Is the principle bound by the acts of the agent? Is there authority? What kind of authority? What are the consequences? If there was implied authority, the principle would be liable under a theory that saw the agent as "transparent." If the agent violated express authority, the principle would be liable, but the principle would be able to bring an action against the agent for breach of the fiduciary duty ...

I was up all night.

By four in the morning, I was paging through the casebook, making sure I was at least familiar with material I had highlighted earlier in the semester. By six I was sketching answers to likely questions and trying to memorize my notes. I was trying to memorize in the car all the way to the exam.

**December 9
(Monday)
(9:00 a.m.)**

For first-year students, the exams at Tulane always begin at one o'clock in the afternoon. In the upper-level classes, the exams begin at nine in the morning. A consistent time made for one less thing to worry about. Most people get to the classroom early and stake out a seat. People who sit in the front of the room all semester suddenly want to sit in the back row. And, of course, until you're seated with your coffee and cache of pens, anything can go wrong. Law students are trained to see every possible misstep. Your car might not start. You might forget your exam number. You might lock your outline in the car. Anything can happen. You're in law school. You know the forces of the universe are often against you.

I arrived at school ten minutes early. The room was already full. The fellow on my left was still thumbing through an outline that looked a hundred pages thick. His name was Peter Ball. Normally he sat in front of me. He took school seriously, I knew, because occasionally he would say something about a good study day.

"You're a Three L," I told him. "What are you worried about?"

"Right now I'm in the top twenty-four percent. I figure, with people working jobs and taking the last year in stride, I might be able to get in the top twenty."

And I was thinking, are those the kind of distinctions I want to live with, having my value as a human being depend on a few percentage points ...

I looked to the woman on my right to see what her outline looked like. She heard our discussion and dropped her thin bundle lightly on the table as if it were a feather floating to earth. "I just put down the stuff Tarenzella says at the beginning of class," she said, "her little wrap-ups."

... Only later did I notice in *The National and Federal Legal Employment Report* that you had to graduate in the top twenty percent of your class to qualify for national attorney placement positions.

So there you go.

Lines were being drawn across our chests.

Shortly before nine, the exam booklets were distributed. Tarenzella said a few words, and students who wanted to smoke or type took their exams to another room.

"It's now nine-o-two," Tarenzella said, checking the clock behind her, and waiting for the second hand to reach twelve. "The exam will end at twelve-o-three.... Begin."

The first thing I did was skim over the exam. Conventional wisdom is to read all of the questions first to make sure you don't go into too much detail on a particular topic when the discussion would have been more appropriate on another question. This was conventional wisdom I usually ignored. I was never one for reading the exam through. When I saw something I could write, I started to write. If I was getting something down on paper, I felt better. The better I felt, the greater chance there was that I would come up with more to say. I thumbed through the B.E. exam just to assure myself that Tarenzella hadn't given us a limited partnership question.

But there it was.

A question allotted thirty minutes of time.

Close to 20 percent of the exam.

So even as I began to write, I was wondering how I could justify a low grade in business. I looked up every time someone opened the door to go to the restroom or return. There went Mark Auburn. The guy walked like his feet were blocks of cement. Grace under pressure. He wasn't going to run. He sidled out the door.... And when I got to the limited partnership question I drew heavily on the code commentary and shot as many arrows as I could, hoping that some would hit the target.

Afterward, I passed on an invitation to go out for a beer and headed home to put my Pollution Control notes into some order. With almost two weeks to go, three exams remaining, I had no clue why I was putting myself through all of this and doubtful whether I could muster the enthusiasm to finish. I had passed B.E., I knew, and had even managed to say the things I wanted to say about agency, but I left with a bitter taste in my mouth.

December 11
(Wednesday)

If there's any intellectualization that goes on in law school, it's during the last couple of weeks before finals when I can put a course together, when I can see how different areas relate and find a few interesting things to say. At the least I try to come up with a way to approach the material. Now I had no time to do anything but reel in my own lack of foresight.

Jonathan came over later that evening. Forced to flee the piles of books and notes from other courses that littered my desk in the kitchen, I had once again set up shop at a card table in the living room, my makeshift headquarters. It was temporary and functional. I placed the table next to a lamp and scattered papers around me on the floor. It would be another long night, but after slugging through two days, I finally had some adrenaline. Only with the exam less than a day away could I get work done at a decent pace, filter through the nonsense, so

I inevitably stayed up all night before exams. Pollution Control would be no different.

Jonathan had apparently just stepped out of the shower. His hair was wet and nicely combed.

"I'm through studying," he said

"I'm not."

Jonathan seemed to prowl around the room. I tried to hide the Nutshell as best I could. It was embarrassing to be seen like this.

"One day," I told Jonathan, "I'll make the perfect outline."

"You're running out of time."

"I'll make the perfect outline, and you know what, I might even memorize it."

"Good luck."

"Did you go out after your criminal procedure exam?" I asked him.

"I went out for a beer. I ended up with a bunch of people I didn't know very well. We didn't discuss the exam. It was nice."

"I heard the exam was easy."

"I stay up late working out the finer points of tangential arguments," he muttered. I figured he was explaining why his lights had been on until two-thirty the night before the exam.

"I'm sure you did well."

"I'm not really interested in criminal procedure," he said. "I just think it would be useful to know what *Miranda* means if it comes up in conversation."

"I never really thought of going to law school as a primer for cocktail party conversation."

"Well ..."

"That's what I'll do after I graduate, I'll start a correspondence course: How to talk like a lawyer in twelve easy steps."

"Yeah."

"You know, like, how to talk trusts to tea clubs."

"Yeah," Jonathan said, moving to my window. "I heard Vice Dean Richards graduated first in his class at Stanford and never went to class."

"Yeah?"

"Is not attending class one of those things where the story just gets more exaggerated as the years go by? I didn't attend much as an undergraduate, but twenty years from now will I be saying I never attended?"

"I can't believe he never attended," I said.

"There are people who never attend. You see them on the last day of class. They show up just to find out what's on the exam."

"If I did anything, I'd go to class. It's so much easier just to find out what the professor wants."

"I wonder what you'd do all day," Jonathan said.

"You'd study."

"Would you work?"

"You'd study."

But Jonathan was still looking out the window, trying to figure out what he'd do all day if he didn't go to school. Rosey liked to call him the reasonable man.

After Jonathan left, I went back to the Nutshell, trying to get the basics of Pollution Control, trying to figure out how I might possibly pass the exam ...

There was a heavy rain that night. I thought for a minute the street might flood. After it let up, a helicopter chortled outside my window, the spotlight swirling on the street. I didn't have to be a lawyer. A law degree would be useful in other areas. A law degree could be useful if I went back into journalism. My ELJ experience would no doubt help. Of course if I wanted a good job, they would look at my grades. It always came down to grades. But I was feeling better just thinking of other prospects. I drafted a letter to the *Village Voice* expressing an interest in a job as a reporter with the paper. Norman Mailer had been one of the paper's founders. The law student meets the champ. He'd like that. Katie and I knew people in New York City. Of course, there were the loans to pay off, but if we both worked and put one of our salaries toward paying off the debt ...

I didn't have time for such thoughts, but I couldn't help myself. Over the past couple of weeks, I had been drawn, more and more, to draft letters to publishing companies, newspapers, magazines, graduate schools ...

It made me feel better.

December 12
(Thursday)
(9:00 a.m.)

By morning, I was quite shaken. The class had failed to take any shape whatsoever, and as a last resort I had made an outline of sorts from my class notes. But I was very uncertain. I hadn't grasped the CAA's approach to Prevention of Significant Deterioration. I hadn't figured out what the material on hazardous air pollutants was all about, even though Muder had all but told us it would be on the exam. And I hadn't even mastered health-based standards, Muder's pet. I hadn't even had time to read her article on the subject.

I looked pretty bad when I got to school. I bought some caffeine in a can and put some peppermints in my mouth. Read the exam. You will have three hours to respond. Allocate your time accordingly. And things did not go well. I was thrown from the first question, apparently about publicly owned treatment works, which Muder had dismissed as rare in comparison to the number of industrial sources of pollution. If I'd had more sleep, better notes, some level of confidence, I would have come up with something intelligent to say. But as it was, the engine just sputtered along in a wake of crossed out sentences. The last question had to do with the pollution crisis in Mexico City. What could be done? A thinker question. A gimme. I would start there. Put a bubble over the city. Cars are the real problem. I just wanted to let her know that I had been to class, that I had learned something. So I put words on paper, double-spaced, wrote on one side of the page, legibly, something, anything, while I watched the time allotted to each question get gobbled up like a cookie.

I wasn't meant to be a lawyer.

December 13
(Friday)

For weeks, every time the telephone rang I thought of Gaines. When the call finally came I was taken by surprise. I picked up the phone and heard the voice of Ivan Mayle introducing himself. He was one of the lawyers with whom I'd had dinner.

"Yes," I said.

"Ivan. From Gaines, Duncan, Duffy & Gray."

"Yes." I felt no emotion. Nothing.

"I'm sorry we've been so long in getting back to you," he explained. "I've been out of town quite a bit lately."

"That's all right."

"Well," he said after a pause, "this is one of those good telephone calls.… We'd like to make you an offer, but I'd like to explain the situation before you make your decision."

"Please." Katie would be happy. My parents would be happy. I was wondering if I could still work for a newspaper part-time over the summer.

"We all had the impression that you were interested in environmental law, and I have to tell you, the firm's environmental law practice has not grown as much as we—as much as I—would have liked, but as of right now, there simply isn't enough work."

"All right."

"The fact is there might not be enough work in environmental law to make you a full-time offer after graduation. I should tell you also, as I'm sure you're aware, hiring is tight all over. Our firm has been luckier than most. We haven't had to lay anyone off, thank God, largely because the people managing the firm have been very conservative. But we don't know where the economy will go—I can't make any guarantees about the firm's needs in the future. We really can't make any hiring commitments at this time."

"I understand that."

"Now, you don't have to decide right now. If you'd like to think about it for awhile, that's fine. I'm sure I've given you a lot to think about."

I had made a mistake the previous year not accepting the offer from Simoneaux on the spot, saying instead that I needed some time to think it over. This time I had Gaines, Duncan, Duffy & Gray tattooed on my chest. "Well, as you say, I've had a lot of time to think about it, and I decided that if I received an offer from Gaines I would accept. You just have to tell me what to do next."

"Well," he said. "Well, that's wonderful. People will be very happy to hear that. Everyone here liked you very much. The next step? I suppose you'll hear from Marie Anderson sometime in the next few weeks."

"Very good."

"I suppose you're getting ready for exams."

"I'm right in the middle of exams, as a matter of fact. I've already had two. I have several more to go."

"Oh, I certainly remember how that is," he said. He sighed. "Getting outlines together and all that. I hope they're going well."

"I think they're going well."

"I'm happy to hear it," he said. "I'd better let you get back to your studies."

"Two more exams and it's back to Columbus."

"Well, be sure to stop by the firm," he said.

I promised I would, and hung up the phone with a strong sense of guilt about the B.E. and Pollution Control exams. This was my chance and I had already let it get away. The grades wouldn't be good, I knew that. The grades on the final two wouldn't be much better. And of course there was Pollution Control. I was supposed to be interested in environmental law. How in the world could I explain a bad grade in Pollution Control? That was the one class in which I was supposed to do well, the one subject I was supposed to like. What if I failed the exam? That was a real possibility. I had scarcely written anything intelligible. I hadn't grappled with a single major issue. The exam was like getting slapped in the face and took about as long. I couldn't show up for work badly bruised and expect to be taken seriously.

But there were other questions to be answered. Katie wanted to know where we'd live, whether we'd still go to Washington. I didn't know. Dad couldn't be reached on the phone. Katie's sister-in-law called, and, although Katie was talking in low tones, I overheard Katie tell her that she might be pregnant. She wasn't supposed to say anything to anyone until she was sure. I scowled at her when she came into the kitchen, but she didn't notice or didn't care.

I went back to the Evidence outline and looked at the words. I thought about going into Gaines over Christmas break to work out the logistics of the summer. I thought about the giant plastic azalea in their lobby. Perhaps word had gotten back that I was interviewing at other law firms in Columbus and Cleveland. Frederick, the environmental lawyer at Fielding, knew people at Gaines. The hiring partner at Branegan, Reed had gone to school with Kimball Donilan. Perhaps someone had seen me at the City Center where I waited for my parents to take me to the airport at the end of that second trip. It would have been clear that I was in town interviewing. It said something that people wanted to speak with me. It said, at least, that I was spending a great deal of money because Gaines had dragged its feet. I had no idea if any of this mattered. I only knew that Gaines had laid the groundwork for not offering me a full-time job and that I had two and a half days to learn Evidence.

I tried to study, but Christmas was already here. I appeared in the doorway to Ivan's office with a suit and a smile and a cheery voice, and he greeted me the same way. We made smalltalk and I looked out his window and neither of us mentioned the poem I had sent him about an owl in the attic.

December 14
(Saturday)

I spent Friday morning polishing a letter to Fielding, a letter that struck the right balance between their loss and my gain. I asked them to kindly keep me in mind for the future. But their letter reached me before I could get mine in the mail:

> Dear Mr. Westphal:
>
> On behalf of the firm, I want to thank you for spending the day with us on December 2.
>
> As you know, we have been fortunate this year to have seen a number of highly qualified candidates. We have thus had many difficult employment decisions to make. As I am sure you realize, the competition for the limited number of positions is quite intense. We enjoyed meeting you and are impressed by your qualifications, but unfortunately we will be unable to extend an offer for a summer position.
>
> Thank you again for your interest in our firm and we wish you every success in the remainder of the school year.
>
> Sincerely,
>
> Jerome P. Thorson
> Recruiting Committee
> Chairman
>
> JPT/jgm

I thought about sending my letter anyway, but finally threw it away and focused on memorizing the outline I had found at the back of my Evidence book. It was a nice straightforward outline that Landrow, if he knew about it at all, hadn't mentioned to the class.

December 16
(Monday)
(9:00 a.m.)

I stumbled through the Evidence exam, afterward grumbling like every else that Louisiana law seemed to play a larger part than we had been led to expect. Hadn't Landrow said it would only amount to about three percent? The oddest part of the morning was the odor of muscle ointment from the guy who sat in front of me. He had smeared himself with the stuff. Some sort of associational thing, I figured, a college athlete reliving glory days. I finally put it out of my mind, sucked on my peppermints, and tried to find a way to say something intelligent on the essay portion.

Jeremy was upbeat afterward. Sharon wasn't so sure. She said a Beatles song had played over and over in her head. She couldn't shake it. Three hours of getting back to where you once belonged.

"That happens to me, too," Jonathan said.

And they carried on a conversation about songs that played in their heads during final exams.

December 18
(Wednesday)

It was almost over. The first semester of my second year of law school was almost over. Only one more exam to go: Remedies. I called Jose the night before to see how his studying was coming along. The first time I tried his number I got his machine. I tried again at about eleven and reached him. He seemed worried as well. He called back several times to see what Worth had said on this or that. I read him whatever I had in my notes. By four o'clock, Jose said he was calling it a night. He couldn't spend all his energy on Remedies; he had another exam on Friday. I told him I would be going to bed soon myself.

At six I was in bed reading when my system just shut down. I became afraid that if I didn't set the alarm, the next thing I'd know it would be ten o'clock, so I set the alarm and shut my eyes. It was a cold night. I huddled beneath the covers. I thought I was going to fail for sure.

December 19
(Thursday)
(9:00 a.m.)

I took a seat at the back of the room and began spreading my notes around me like sandbags in a bunker. I would write something. I would copy my notes if I had to. I just wanted to spot an issue or two and I'd write what I had prepared. At least I had come to class. A number of people hadn't been seen since the beginning of the semester.

Worth was fluttering about the front of the room. Exam day is usually like a day off for the professor, a Saturday at the office. Most wear jeans, something casual, but Worth was wearing what he wore every day, a dark charcoal suit, pink shirt, and floral tie.

"As some of you may know," he said, "due to the beneficence of a Tulane alumnus, and to encourage Remedies scholarship, an award has been established for the best exam written in this class. It's fairly substantial. One thousand dollars ... if that provides incentive for any of you to give your exam a bit more thought than you might have otherwise."

Worth smirked more than usual. Incentive. It was typical, I thought, that we were told such things only when it was too late to do anything about it. Well, this was certainly an award I wouldn't win. I was hoping just to find something to say for the next three hours ... which is what I did, crossing out a page I had written on the second question, a false start, and finishing the last question, asking us to reflect on the current state of Remedies, with the notion that the state of Remedies wasn't bad considering we were on a rock hurling through space. It was an idea that wouldn't win points with a judge, but Worth might get a kick out of it. One lunatic to another.

Worth reappeared at the end of the exam, fluttering again as the exam booklets were turned in. He made me nervous. Jose shook his hand. The two seemed like old friends.

Outside, I stopped to drink champagne with some people in front of the law school. These people drank champagne at the end of each semester. I sat on the steps and had a glass just to feel the effect. Worth went streaking past in his suit with a briefcase full of exams.

It was all over.

The semester was over.

*   *   *

The next day Katie and I would leave for Columbus. I stood at my locker at school removing books and papers. After all the flush and fury, I felt suddenly empty. I put my notes into file folders and labeled them. I had the idea I would read them again when it came time to study for the bar exam. I stopped once to read the sample answer to one of Muder's old exams. I hadn't had time to look at it before. It could have helped, I thought. It could have provided a practical approach to problems that to me were never more than abstract concepts. My problem was that I never knew the material until the last minute. This semester there had been casenotes, contests, committees, airplanes and interviews, and no last minute.

*   *   *

I walked slowly down the street toward my car. I had a wife, a baby on the way, a job lined up. My life was advancing rapidly in ways I couldn't comprehend. Commitments were being made. I wondered if I would ever be able to put it together into a meaningful whole. I would get through law school. I would be a lawyer. I would wear a suit, sit in an office, and deal out my time like playing cards. That's what I would do. Thoreau left Walden Pond because he had other lives to lead. From where I stood, breaking away from the law seemed about as likely as catching a loon. I would be a lawyer. Many had tried and failed. Many more had not tried at all. I would be a lawyer. That made a difference somehow. That gave me comfort. That gave me determination. That helped to set my course.

As I passed the site of the new chemistry building, the construction workers were eating lunch, sitting near the fence in dirty jeans and tarnished white helmets. A lot of workers, a lot of money, and still just a lot of rubble. Construction costs money. Someone was paying. Another day, another few thousand dollars. A drop in the bucket on a $25 million project. For a moment, I almost understood the fees lawyers charge. A securities offering? You'll be a millionaire overnight. You want to acquire a company? It should shore up your product line and provide a hedge against recessionary forces. A few thousand here, a few thousand there. Lawyers' fees, just the cost of doing business, just the cost of construction. Soon there would be a building standing so high it would make you gasp. Just the necessary cost of construction.

I don't know how long I stood there, staring up at the sky.

Epilogue

Each semester in law school was a little different, but each had at least one thing in common. When exams were over, it always seemed as if I had eaten the meal so fast I could hardly remember what had been put in my mouth. Fine delineations, whole concepts, even common sense principles seemed to disappear as I walked out the door. What remained were a few jokes, some peculiar facial expressions, sometimes a question asked or the facts of a particular case. Some classes seemed to reduce to a single sentence. Contracts: You get what you pay for. Family Law: Tit for tat. Conflicts: You play in my yard, you play by my rules.

I went home at the end of the first semester of my second year carrying little bits of energy, doubt, knowledge, wisdom. Listening to Landrow, the adversarial process hardly seemed, as Wigmore had said, the greatest engine of truth known to man. In Remedies, an injury was often only as good as its cause was bad. Business Enterprises helped the rich get richer. And the Clean Water Act was a big cork with a few holes, more problematic than utopic, soaked in scientific uncertainty.

I returned to school after a break far too short and settled in with classes, with my work on the ELJ. Grades finally began to trickle out in late January and February. As I suspected, the limited partnership question on the B.E. exam was damaging. Still, I ended up with B's in both Business and Remedies. Landrow's crazy point system and the Louisiana law got the best of me: C+. The worst, though, was Pollution

Control, where in February I found facing me on the weeping wall a big fat C. I wasn't going to quibble. There were plenty of other C's, several D's. Some people, I was told, had written notes to Muder on their exams: I really came to class, I really listened, I really studied. They really had. They just hadn't studied the right way. To do well on exams, you have to have the material ready to spill out on the page. You have to walk into the room like a barrel full of water and be careful not to trip on the way to your seat.

It takes so long for grades to be posted that by the time they were in I could almost see summer. More than halfway through law school, I could finally look ahead to some day when there would be cakes and cards and money coming through the mail. Jonathan would cut his ponytail. Jose would still need notes. A song about a baby bumblebee would echo in my head as I wrote my last exam. And some day, some day soon, I would blink my eyes and twenty-five years would be gone. Look. There I go, walking home from work on a cold November evening along the dark streets of Columbus, Ohio, my charcoal overcoat flapping about my legs and my breath coming out in spurts. I see it now, the trees along the curb, my little brick house in German Village, the shiny red truck in the driveway across the street. It is cold and dark and I am walking home, Katie ahead, already standing on the stoop, fumbling for keys.

This is my life. I have a reputation for writing briefs that smash high-priced lawyers into little pieces. At times, I enjoy my work. I have an office. I have a desk. I have learned by experience that often in life there are no alarms, no buzzers, no sprinklers going off overhead. I burst through emergency exits with the confidence of a lawyer. Then I march back into the library and begin again the next day.

This is my life, and there is no one to blame but myself. So I move down the street toward home, the bottom of my charcoal overcoat coursing with each step, Katie already inside. There I go, hands in pockets, slouching toward my destiny.

About the Author

Lawrence Dieker Jr. graduated with honors from Tulane Law School. He practices law in Ohio, where he lives with his wife and their three children.

Printed in the United States
1188100003B/41